THE
YOLO
PAGES

ISBN : 0996069100
ISBN-13 : 978-0-9960691-0-6

www.boost-house.com
facebook.com/boost.house
boosthouse.tumblr.com
twitter.com/boosthouse
instagram.com/boosthouse

info@boost-house.com

INTRODUCTION 5

ADEFISAYO ADEYEYE 13
BEACH SLOTH 17
GABBY BESS 22
LIZ BOWEN 26
MELISSA BRODER 29
JOS CHARLES 31
RICHARD CHIEM 36
SANTINO DELA 39
BRIAN ECKLUND 42
PANCHO ESPINOSA 44
JOSHUA JENNIFER ESPINOZA 47
CATALINA GALLAGHER 52
JAMES GANAS 58
CEAN GAMALINDA 65
CASSANDRA GILLIG 68
AMELIA GILLIS 71
LARA GLENUM 75
PHILIP GORDON 77
TOM HANK 79
MICHAEL HESSEL-MIAL 83
@HORSE_EBOOKS 88
BRETT ELIZABETH JENKINS 93
RAYMOND JOHNSON 95
KENJI KHOZOEI 99
JI YOON LEE 102
TAO LIN 104
CAYLA LOCKWOOD 108

PATRICIA LOCKWOOD 111
CARRIE LORIG 116
STEPHEN MICHAEL MCDOWELL 118
SHARON MESMER 123
LUNA MIGUEL 128
K. SILEM MOHAMMAD 131
MOON TEMPLE 134
ASHLEY OPHEIM 136
ANTHONY PEREGRINE 142
@POSTCRUNK 146
JOHN ROGERS 151
AMY SAUL-ZERBY 156
BOB SCHOFIELD 159
LK SHAW 162
ANGELA SHIER 166
BIANCA SHIPTON 171
ALLI SIMONE DEFEO 176
ANDREW W.K. 178
SARA WOODS 181
DYLAN YORK 184

BOOST HOUSE TEAM:
CHARLIE THE DOG EMERITUS 188
JOSEPH KENDRICK 190
STEVE ROGGENBUCK 193
E.E. SCOTT 197
RACHEL YOUNGHANS 200

LINK APPENDIX 203
COVER BY HUNTER PAYNE.

with *the yolo pages* we wanted to demonstrate the incredible energy and variety that exists in poetry in 2014. having inherited a tradition of open formal experimentation from the postmodern era, and now inheriting an ongoing stream of additional new forms from the internet, poetry is far more exciting today than most people have been letting on.

especially where poetry has moved onto the internet, things are developing very quickly and most publishers have been slow to cover it. looking over a recent poetry anthology that claimed to include "cyberpoetry" and "digital poetry," we found its youngest contributor was 35 years old. in contrast, roughly half the contributors of this book are under 25 at the time of publishing, having grown up with the internet as an integral part of their lives.

loosely this is a poetry anthology—yet it contains more tweets than it does conventional-looking poems. we've included visual poems in styles reminiscent of lol cats, photos of handwriting, poster designs, and snapchats. we've included poems that use various forms and methods from the modern and postmodern avant-gardes. bred to catch attention in a noisy online environment, the poetry in this book is visual, contemporary, and aggressively engaging.

we've included figures who write under pseudonyms like beach sloth, moon temple, and tom hank. we've included figures widely known for their tweets: @horse_ebooks, @tricialockwood, @santinodela, and @postcrunk. and in that same spirit of looking outside of "poetry" to find poetry, we've included writing by the musician andrew w.k., as well as fiction writer richard chiem and numerous people working in multiple or hybrid artforms.

the avant-gardes of the 20th century pushed poetry so far in so many directions. our inheritance now and forever is the ongoing uncertainty of what "poetry" is. if all our old definitions of poetry have been smashed apart, then in 2014 we get to define for ourselves: what will participating in poetry mean for us? what does it mean to be a poet now?

on the "alt lit" community

not exactly an "alt lit anthology," this book claims to cover "alt lit" for one of the first times in an anthology. but the term "alt lit" has proven highly contentious and hard to define. what are we exactly referring to?

to the best of our knowledge, the term "alt lit" was coined by cory stephens (@outmouth) in the summer of 2011. cory's use of the word "alt" was influenced by the blog *hipster runoff*, which often referred to hipsters and indie youth as "alts." around this same time, cory was also referring to almond milk and soy milk as "alt milk." given this backstory, it feels strange when people say "alternative literature" like it's the proper, full version of the name. from the beginning it was "alt lit," essentially meaning "hipster lit."

the writers originally grouped under the "alt lit" label had previously been collected to some degree by *pop serial*, muumuu house, *internet poetry*, and *htmlgiant*, among other venues. there had been a bit of an online scene for this indie lit for a few years, without any label for it. cory started an *alt lit gossip* tumblr to cover these "alt lit" writers in a style similar to *tmz* writing about celebrities. after a few months cory abandoned the tumblr, and then canadian writer frank hinton squatted on the name and web address to continue the blog. it was mainly her advocacy in late 2011 that got the name to catch on.

in 2012 the term "alt lit" spread quickly. countless new lit mags poured out of the community, only a few of which would have staying power—*shabby doll house*, *have u seen my whale*, and *illuminati girl gang* among them. spreecast and ustream were often used for online poetry readings, and it became common for "alt lit" writers to have 100+ mutual facebook friends with each other, most of whom had never met in person. many blogs became focused on sharing "alt lit" links, reviews, and interviews. these blogs included *beach sloth*, *i am alt lit*, *alt lit press*, *cutty spot*, and *alt lit library*. by mid-2012, the ubitiquity of "alt lit" itself became entertaining enough to spawn the creation of blogs like *i am not alt lit* and *alt lit gossip 2*

in early 2013 the "alt lit" community earned a long, insulting article from *vice magazine* and, soon after, inclusion on the website *know your meme*. despite all this hype, or maybe because of it, writers very rarely self-identify with the term "alt lit" seriously. the original community has expanded rapidly and fractured into numerous sub-groups. even as the tumblr tag "alt lit" gains widespread use by young poets, almost everyone seriously associated with the term has questioned it or distanced themself from it at some time. all uses of "alt lit" in this book are placed in quotation marks to reflect how self-aware our use of the term is.

to describe "alt lit" writing is difficult because when writers get labeled "alt lit," it's ultimately because of where they've published and who they're friends with—not their writing style. there's been a widespread use of image macros as a literary form in "alt lit," for example, but prominent community members have also decried that fact. critics often point to "ennui" and "nihilism" in "alt lit," but in fact many of the writers grapple with death and limited time in a way that's deeply spiritual. interest in buddhism seems especially common, but again—there's so many exceptions. the main shared value is just an embrace of the internet as a tool for making and distributing literature.

the yolo pages doesn't seek to be a full-on "alt lit" anthology. we've left out many of the major "alt lit" figures, while including some poets entirely separate from that scene. we've included poets who belong much more to "weird twitter," another contentious grouping of writers, which is maybe a sister community to "alt lit," as well as a couple of flarf poets, and many more with no clear affiliation. overall we hope to showcase a smattering of compelling new forms and trends, regardless of community ties. as a part of that effort, we're honored to help shed light on the "alt lit" world now, before its historical importance is recognized more widely.

the most yolo poetry anthology

cataloging all this exciting new poetry would be purpose enough for this anthology to exist. but we also wanted to tint our selections in a certain direction as we pulled from "alt lit" and other communities. we wanted to present a disproportionate amount of socially-, politically-, and spiritually-minded poets. we wanted to focus the most on poets who are hungry to change the world—to criticize oppressive systems, and use their art and the connective power of social media to make things better in some way—at the very least, to spread warmth and kindness through these platforms.

the word "yolo" in this book's title is meant to invoke a "carpe diem" impulse that goes back through over 2,000 years of literature. in 23 bce, the latin poet horace wrote, "carpe diem, quam minimum credula postero" ("sieze the day, trusting as little as possible in the next"). in 2011 ce, drake wrote "yolo." an acronym for "you only live once," yolo is routinely dismissed as a trivial, often reckless youth meme. in fact people have died from actions taken immediately after saying "yolo."

but we've also seen "yolo" bring out in people a real and important appreciation for their limited time on earth. saying "yolo" can be a way of invoking a deeply spiritual subject—human mortality and our reaction to it—in a fun and unintimidating way. saying "yolo" can become an excuse to live now, to do what we really want today because we might not get another day.

most importantly we think "yolo" can provide a passion and sense of agency that encourages us to say and do what we really believe in, ethically. if we only live once, there's no time for half-assing things, accepting unfulfilled potential, or being complicit with systems that actually disgust us. if we think something is wrong, then we should act to stop it. recognizing our limited time on earth can give us strength in that effort. several writers in this book push forward this understanding of "yolo" in their work.

toward a broader understanding of "political poetry"

too often our conceptions of "political poetry" are so narrow they mainly only include one kind of poem. such political poems directly show us the brutality of something like military occupation, gender-based violence, or environmental destruction, and they call us to help change the situation. those poems are valuable, and you'll find a few in this book. but if you consider all the ways social change can happen, all the ways individuals can be moved to take various sorts of action, then "political poetry" can become a much broader category.

think about the politics of something like making vegan cupcakes. no one is immediately shutting down a slaughterhouse by baking them. and yet, we've known people who only went vegan upon realizing the wealth of vegan baked goods available. vegan cupcakes help create a vegan subculture that's fun enough for people to get excited about it. to make our activist efforts sustainable, we need culture to celebrate and enjoy along the way. for everything we boycott or oppose, we need to find (or create) a wealth of ethical alternatives.

so in a world where mainstream culture is tinged with varying amounts of racism, sexism, classism, ableism, homophobia, and transphobia, it becomes valuable simply to form communities and collections of writing where those ideas aren't tolerated. to create beautiful or funny poetry that is merely *compatible with* anti-oppression politics may even contribute to the well-being of fellow activists. even better is to create writing that reflects a worldview where such activism is celebrated or affirmed as part of the status quo of that community.

buddhist monk thich nhat hanh refers to "engaged buddhism" as a spiritual path that includes social activism as an integral part. if compassion and nonviolence are important to us spiritually, then we should take concrete steps to stop violence in the world as well. what good is inner peace or personal happiness if you turn a cheek from those suffering around you? the best "positivity" helps us to stay hopeful and energized in the struggle for a better world.

you'll find that most poets in this book are at least loosely aligned with some activist work—it shows in certain tweets or poems, even if the rest of the work addresses other concerns. this kind of work promotes an integration of radical politics into the fabric of one's life and culture. we don't write a single "political poem" once a year like a check sent to a charity each winter, but instead engage social and political concerns on an ongoing basis in the main text, right alongside subjects like love, work, friendship, and death. this work recognizes the power of poetry to transform peoples' consciousness in a holistic way, in a way distinct from but complementary to more direct calls to action.

at the beginning of boost house

the yolo pages also has a role as a statement of intention at the beginning of boost house. this is the first book produced by boost house as a group effort. boost house is a publisher and residency started this year in brunswick, maine. our initial team is four humans and a dog—we've included a section of our own creative work in this book, starting on page 188. in the future we hope to expand to support many more artists and activists with residencies and publications.

the concerns of this book—internet-based poetry, yolo spirituality, and radical politics—are ongoing concerns for boost house. we intend to publish many of the poets in this book at more length in the future. we hope this book will inspire and cross-connect many likeminded writers and readers coming to it from separate ways. if you like someone's work, please find their web presence (the appendix includes a list) and reach out to them! when we build community like this, everyone benefits.

thank you friend for your support at the beginning of boost house. we are very excited to be doing this work, and even more excited to share it with you.

<3
steve roggenbuck, editor.
e.e. scott, editor.
rachel younghans, editor.
april 2014

"the poet or the revolutionary is there to articulate the necessity, but until the people themselves apprehend it, nothing can happen ... perhaps it can't be done without the poet, but it certainly can't be done without the people. the poet and the people get on generally very badly, and yet they need each other. the poet knows it sooner than the people do. the people usually know it after the poet is dead; but that's all right. the point is to get your work done, and your work is to change the world."

james baldwin

MOONMOTH

December 2028:

The sky is an unpolished thing.
The sky has frosted around your lips
and your mouth looks like a flower.

I eat your flower lips.
I call you my mouth.

I taste you tomorrow.

December 2013:

The house sits behind us.
There are ants climbing up and down a blade
of grass

I want to touch you but if I touch you
I want to know if it will be like I didn't ever
touch you

we are sitting in the middle of the earth
we are sitting right at the center
we are sitting right on top of it.

Can you feel us?
How much would you weigh
without us?

December 2013:

The house is telling stories about
the people inside its head.

The moon is moving or the earth
or the sky something is moving
we are not moving

when you broke your spine I was
the one you spilled into

when I vomited up my heart
you were the one who packaged it

we are enjoying being responsible
for each others madness.

December 2000:

I kiss you to taste your
reflection.

I kiss you to taste you inverted.

December 2013:

The house looks sad because
there are ants all over the porch.

Last night we tried to bleach the sadness
out of our skins.
We did laundry all night hung the sheets
from the lines and they flapped uselessly against
the sky.

The sun was filming us.
It wanted to remember this.

MOUTHFULS

I can't open my mouth because I will cover you with   stars

I can swim in my own amniotic fluid   probably

my stained red teeth can eat glass out of your   crucified palms

and bury things in you

tomorrow we will hold funerals for   tiny voices
tomorrow we will hold funerals for   tiny voices
tomorrow

    I will be jealous of

              our tiny tiny red mouths

              kissing the

                  black of it all

  jealous of the people   able to say

stop

    jealous of the people   able to say

tomorrow we will hold funerals for   tiny voices

                  they will be beautiful   (and
             all of them

will be beautiful)

UNTITLED

///////Prayers,

                              I am asking you

          Lips.

I am kissing you.

                              /////////Remotely

my tongue, the inside

                    of your sat—

          ellite////////////

adefisayo adeyeye was born in 1990 and currently lives in southern california. his work engages with the juxtaposition between the cosmically big and the infinitely small. adefisayo is a student and a poetry editor for *amorphous magazine*. he like whales. he seems to like whales a lot.

HEY YOU

You are sitting at a desk different from mine. Maybe
You are lying down or maybe
You are reading this on a phone or maybe
You are right in front of me I'm uncertain. What I am certain of is
You are wonderful
You have a lot going for
You
You will achieve all your dreams
You know what to do
You say such nice things
You never put other people down
You lift them up
You are a beam of light piercing through cloudy days
You are one of my favorite people. Nobody is quite like You
You are unique out of billions of people as
You are reading this right now. Thank
You for tuning into my little corner of the universe maybe
	someday
You will see me
You will sit across from me in the train
You will not recognize me and I will not recognize
You but the anonymous support we give each other is
enough. I care deeply about
You and hope we meet and never know it.

 **BeachSloth**
@Beach_Sloth

LinkedIn Park

 BeachSloth
@Beach_Sloth

Walden is an American Instagram Filter created by noted transcendentalist Henry David Thoreau

 **BeachSloth**
@Beach_Sloth

Whenever you ask yourself "Am I good enough?" know that you are

 **BeachSloth**
@Beach_Sloth

A TED talk about being a privileged piece of shit

BeachSloth
@Beach_Sloth

A Ted Talk that consists of the speaker laughing at the audience the entire time

18

BeachSloth
@Beach_Sloth

Beards are the welcome mats of the face

BeachSloth
@Beach_Sloth

The internet is not a cold, dark place.

BeachSloth
@Beach_Sloth

Wait until I fuck Santa Claus in his ass

BeachSloth
@Beach_Sloth

Every time I am away from the internet I wonder if I am loved

BeachSloth
@Beach_Sloth

Pay attention to today because today is beautiful

BeachSloth
@Beach_Sloth

It doesn't matter what you look like on the outside it's what's on the internet that counts

19

It is important to remember what wonderful creatures share the world with humans. Humans do not own the world. Thus it is critical that humans treat other creatures with respect. No creature is above the other except for trees. Trees are really tall.

▲

"Every new beginning comes from some other beginning's end." - Plato

▲

Had Jesus invited me to the Last Supper I would've been like "Oh sweet free food"

▲

I never got into Donnie Darko because I was post-emo by the time emo happened.

▲

Exploring the worst negative impulses is considered 'high art'. Being happy is considered 'low art' or comedy. Yet there is nothing easy about finding happiness.

Beach Sloth
February 19

I wish I could be as beautiful as the world around me but I'm starting to think that's not possible. Every day I wake up and my heart hurts for the world. The things I see wherever I go are incredible. What people have done for me absolutely mystifies me. Sometimes I wonder when I'll be able to give back to everybody who has been so infinitely kind to me. I'm not sure if I'll ever be able to do it, to accurately express the extreme gratitude I feel towards anybody who does the simplest of tasks for me, who opens up a door, who says nice things when they would be just as fine telling me how to get to the room, or the floor, or when the person will be arriving. Tiny kindnesses mean so much to me and I'm pumping my little insignificant heart every day hoping that those miniscule pumps make a difference for at least one person. That is all I want to do with my life, I just hope one day I'll be able to do it.

beach sloth was born in 1973 and currently lives in new york city. when asked to summarize his worldview in one sentence, he said, "support each other." most of the writers in this book have been reviewed once or more on beach sloth's blog. his "reviews" are often a form of poetry themselves, as he riffs on subjects in the original work more than evaluating it. one the kindest, most generous characters online, beach sloth embodies the open warmth that has made "alt lit" a welcoming space for so many young people to share their creative work.

21

MINIATURE BEARS

On a bed we sit like miniature bears.
You can bury me in your mattress,
I want to sit next to you
until we become dangerous.
Until we become parade balloons of bears,
cut loose and floating too close
to the street level floors of buildings.

"I want you up there,"
you said with closed eyes, pointing
to the chandelier that you called a 'ceiling necklace'.
Cross your heart and hope to live for a very long time.

TOP SITES ON THE WEBSITE LITEROTICA.COM

01 mad thumbs
02 teeniesxxx
03 only movies
04 sublime directory
05 sleezy dreams xxx
06 teenie files
07 voyeurweb
08 dr. bizzaro
09 free voyeurZine
10 tommy's bookmarks
11 old 69 tgp
12 tags portal
13 persian kitty
14 green guy links
15 richard's realm

Gabby Bess
@seemstween

imagined a fictitious rapper called 'lil bouncy' whose gimmick was that he wore chains made out bouncy balls and didn't actually rap

Gabby Bess
@seemstween

brunch is similar to feminism in that it feels like people are talking about it ALL THE TIME but really its just you & your 3 friends

Gabby Bess
@seemstween

dad sent me an email from his iPhone then I replied & then he replied from his iPad, which I didn't kno he had. felt shocked & a little hurt

Gabby Bess
@seemstween

I have this screenshot of Kim Kardashians ass from her Instagram on my phone and I feel hesitant to delete it bc it seems like 'all I have'

Gabby Bess
@seemstween

non-humorously thought, 'I have a thousand crying white girls in me'

Gabby Bess
@seemstween

overheard someone in the office having a crisis about the internet, ending in admitting they have 'tried to go offline' but they 'just cant'

Gabby Bess
@seemstween

RT if u miss my boyfriend

Gabby Bess
@seemstween

lost all of my tweet drafts in the fire...

Gabby Bess
@seemstween

it is a very exciting time right now to be a woman with internet access

24

social networking

gabby bess was born in 1992 and currently lives in new york city. gabby is the author of the poetry and short story collection *alone with other people* and the curator of *illuminati girl gang*, a publication that highlights female artists working within the context of internet culture. currently, her work is focused on the labor of feminine performance in literature and art.

YOLO IS FOR EVERY BODY
(SOME THOUGHTS ON POSITIVITY & DISABILITY)

i am a person with a chronic illness, and i also believe strongly in YOLO. i feel the urgent joy that comes with knowing we are not guaranteed to exist beyond the now, and i worry about the oppressive nature of a life structured by society's expectations. but sometimes this is complicated for me because my life with a disability doesn't always lend itself to spontaneity, which seems like a pretty core tenet of the YOLO/positive philosophy. i have type 1 diabetes, meaning my life depends on a lot of tedious structure: constantly being aware of my blood sugar, carrying three medical devices everywhere i go, inserting tubes under my skin several times a week, calculating the carbs in every piece of food i eat, etc etc. it's similar to the most boring data-entry job, but one in which i also occasionally feel so weak it's like my body is being crushed by a slowly moving cop on a segway.

spur-of-the-moment activities can be difficult for a lot of people with bodily or mental differences, such as people with limited mobility who can't count on spaces being accessible, or people whose chronic anxiety can make it impossible to leave the house. it can be hard to be energized about seizing this life when it feels like your body is sabotaging you, or society is sabotaging you because of your body. that's a reality that shouldn't be ignored. but it's also why YOLO is especially important for me, and possibly for other people with disabilities: knowing my time alive is precious has allowed me to live in this body without apology, regardless of sickness or stigma.

YOLO can look different for those of us with bodily demands that other people might not have, but that doesn't diminish its effect. for me, YOLO doesn't look like the dream of quitting my desk job and couchsurfing across the world, because my survival depends on keeping a job that provides health insurance. but

26

that's ok! because instead, YOLO has meant letting go of shame that i once felt about my body. it's meant testing my blood sugar openly and not caring if people stare, or writing about this major part of my life i was once afraid to talk about, or not giving a fuck when there's a picture of me on facebook that shows my insulin pump. i also envision YOLO to mean demanding equal access to spaces where we should all be equally able to go hard! e.g. advocating for better wheelchair access to music venues or art spaces, or pushing for American Sign Language classes in schools. YOLO has made me realize that viewing my disabled body as 'less than,' something to be hidden or forced to fit others' vision of normal, is truly not worth my time on this earth.

in the spirit of 'YOLO = making good use of our time alive,' i also believe YOLO can (and should) mean taking care of ourselves and each other. how magnificent can this one life be if we're sacrificing our health, or if we don't have communities to support us in moments of darkness? i don't claim to speak for all people with disabilities, but in my own life, i reject the idea that dependence on medical regimens or reliance on disability accommodations rules out the YOLO philosophy. to the contrary, caring for our bodies and inhabiting accessible spaces allows us to live fully in the present, as the people we are.

for every human being — disabled or able-bodied — uninhibited love and community are things we owe ourselves and each other. they are emblematic of YOLO: extreme and intensely positive! uninhibited love means caring for your own body and advocating for its needs, as well as the needs of others, even if it's difficult. so it's worth our time as alive, sentient, empathetic humans to confront our negative feelings about bodily differences and start the endless work of extracting them. it's worth our time to battle bureaucracies that don't want to improve disability accommodations in schools and workplaces. it's worth it to think hard about the way we use words like 'retarded' and 'lame.' it's worth it to ask tough questions about our preconceptions of people whose bodies don't mirror our own.

some people find it easy to get disenchanted with 'positive thinking' in the face of a society that marginalizes anyone perceived to be different, and i understand that. i personally have felt disenchanted more times than i can count. but i struggle less with those feelings when i believe in a positive philosophy that acknowledges the contradiction — that realizes happiness is not always easy and that inequality is real, but that the collective hard work to create positive change is worth it, and is positive in itself.

of course, sometimes you have to take a break from the work, and then you YOLO by running as far into a field as you can, or screaming your favorite song out a car window, or any other bold bright thing that makes you happy! but it would be a mistake to think those bursting moments of joy are all there is to positivity. it might seem like hard work is contradictory to YOLO, and that happiness can't come out of conversations and actions that make us uncomfortable. but if the end result of those actions is a world where more people feel empowered, it's absolutely worth the struggle. if the work is worth the short time we spend alive with each other, it's YOLO.

liz bowen was born in 1990 and currently lives in new york city. she is an incoming doctoral student in english at columbia university with a passion for radical activism, especially on issues of disability and lgbt rights, income inequality, veganism and the prison-industrial complex. liz writes because she believes "it's important that people with disabilities, particularly women and multiply marginalized people, make our experiences heard and fight for a more inclusive language, since most of the writing that does exist about us is just that: about us rather than by us."

WATERFALL

The most romantic thing a human being can say
to another human being is *Let me help you vomit.*
No human being has ever said this to me
and I keep going to god too clean as though god
is frightened of muddy feet. If I am missing
a hairpin I don't go at all. Please describe
your vomiting; it is like a psalm to me
a place where wilderness might be new.
Other people's dirt makes a lovely frock.
Grant I be forgiven in the gush.

BYE

When I die I regret the dieting
and literary theory. I am just
oh my god one raspberry left. Strange
how we had different experiences.
I would love to have handed you toilet paper
under a stall door. I was thinking with my head
and forgot about my hands. I also regret
the obsessing over ragged seams.
Funny thing is: sometimes the obsessing
called attention to itself doing it
while it did it. I guess we could have gone
naked. Do you know the story of Helen?

IT IS GOOD

It is good for the sky
to fall down around you

and good for the wrong plants
to grow in your houseplants

strange plants
mushrooms even

but it would be a lie
if I said that the heart

is not made out of meat
a fat and fatal core

where ether is everywhere
and electricity bends

I do not know why
we cannot

make the whole
story up.

melissa broder currently lives in venice, california. she is the author of multiple poetry collections including *scarecrone* and *meat heart.* she's summarized her own poetry as saying, essentially, "DICK PUSSY HORSES BLOOD HORSES GOD DICK." she runs a popular twitter account and struggles with the difficulty of living in a body.

FROM LOVE LETTERs

Žižek was a 80s pop psychologist whose most famous work is a video about love and toilets.

In this way Žižek is not dissimilar to Hugh Grant.

Love as a means of aestheticizing mortal relationships is a product of some historically brutal shit.

It's old news marriage as a social phenomenon is one of the cruelest interrogations of the social, which from the colonialist hegemony of White Christianity brought 'here', wherein 'here' is coextensive with 'us', is constructed as work ethic, noble, a mobile deserving, establishment of individuality, that is, claim to territory (*to terror to terror to terror*).

Thought, *let go of my ego*.

Thought, *I will do anything for love*.

Thought, *O god I have access to love both as a conceptual framework and as a tool of material distribution*.

What gets left: reserve. The asshole who gets it: economy.

John Donne would say something about suffering.

John Donne had everything going for him in terms of identity and was a miserable shitbaby.

In this way *Love Actually* did something right by substituting *Christmas* for *love* in its dumbass theme song. *Merry Christmas*, like most things, is a way of saying *I love you*.

I love you is the most political shit anyone can say to anybody.

The trick is who is the *you* of the internet vs. the *you* lapping salt water at the beach.

You know who I mean.

I mean no one says *I love you* without saying something else.

No one says *I love you* alone.

/ /

Like a good witch, I write love letters to the night sky.
Don't forget to write! the night sky tells me.

I begin my letters wherever I can.

Dear Los Angeles, I write,

*I will be in the day sky by the time you read this. Right now I am
physically the closest I have ever been to the all-at-once of you.*

*Remember, no matter how close you get to the thing you can
still be filled with longing.*

Sincerely yours,

Jos

It's important to end in earnest. It's the end of things that
matters.

Like when the old sage said *a man broke into your home* he
meant your heart, and when *it turns out he stole everything*, he
meant, especially, the moon.

/ /

The darkness lifts, imagine, in your lifetime.

You've learned to forget the words and know something of the freedom in finitude.

You step out on the lawn. The grass grows high beneath your feet.

The neighbors shut themselves in or leave for friends with willing smiles.

The broken bike has been lifted and you're hands are full and dry.

You learn to forget the old names.

You are, at last, what you never set out to be.

Beauty never enters it.

You stop, look towards the horizon, and praise the strawberry.

The morning she left your father brought you fresh berries from the hotel continental breakfast.

You have daddy issues and he's an asshole.

There needn't be wonder to the sweetness.

There needn't be clearing to feel the moss.

Oh lowly strawberry, you say, *at least for now there is only praise.*

Jos Charles
@josdcharles

I CAN'T COME TO DINNER MOM IM
SOLVING HOMOPHOBIA ON THE
INTERNET

Jos Charles
@josdcharles

well son, me and your father got married
mostly to create jobs

Jos Charles
@josdcharles

if you're able, don't use 'crippling' as a
metaphor. if you're white, don't use 'slavery'
as a metaphor. its v easy

Jos Charles
@josdcharles

i am politically opposed to adults

jos charles was born in 1988 and currently lives in los angeles.
jos is the founding editor of *them*, the first trans literary journal
in the united states. jos is a vegan who goes bananas for john
donne. jos recently bought overalls and is rebranding hir aesthetic
to giant baby. jos's work deconstructs the mom/giant baby binary.

FROM HOW TO SURVIVE A CAR ACCIDENT

Say "yes" when James invites you to L.A. with him for a weekend. Ask what kind of people are going to be there. Walk with your hands in your pockets and realize that you don't know James very well. Feel a warm and mutual respect because you have read his poems in class before and liked the one about the boy who eats a mocking bird. Have conversations about life and death and joke about it. Ask how did that topic come up in the first place. Comment on his black fedora, that you think you like black fedoras.

Meet Jenny in a vacant parking lot, still blue colored from morning light. Look at her in the eyes because she is important to you. Lay on the roof of the car waiting for James in front of his house. Listen to Wu – Tang Clan vibrate the metal of the roof you're laying on. Imagine sitting inside a plane when one flies overhead. You could hear the drug-induced non-anxiety coating James's voice when he wonders where his keys are.

Take the I – 5 North towards L.A. / San Bernardino. Sit shotgun and get assigned to be DJ. Listen to the calming clicks from your iPod. Take peppermint gum from Jenny. Acknowledge you have never done anything with these two friends before. Jenny appears glowing while driving. James in the backseat sinks into the cushion, closes his eyes.

Open and close windows. Talk about past relationships and laugh in unison during sexual parts. Get distracted with other passengers on the highway. Imagine relationships with those that make eye contact with you. Try, and remember Mary in a positive way and cut wind with your hand through your open window.

Play Bon Iver. Light a cigarette to share around with everyone else in the car. Take unconscious drags of smoke.

Slowly pass a sixteen wheeler semi truck on your right hand side. Listen to Skinny Love. Notice a car up ahead swerving into your lane. Watch the car swerve back quickly to its own lane. Exhale when Jenny reacts and turns the steering wheel closer towards you. Hold the armrest while your own car swerves out of control. Notice how calm your breath is. Let things happen. Swerve into the semi on your right. Crash with the momentum of the cabin and everything behind you. Close your eyes. Duck somehow. The roof above you caves down and down again. The noise is tremendous. Glass shatters and rains in small bits and pieces and falls on top of yours and your friends' jeans.

Realize the car is stuck underneath the semi. Get dragged underneath while the semi is braking on the I – 5 North.

Lose your glasses. See blurry and near sighted. Leave the car through Jenny's driver's side door and keep walking away. Feel a strange urge to keep walking away. Resolve to baby steps. Jenny is ahead and James is behind you. Ask if everyone is okay with your mouth.

Hear your friends say your name a few times. Watch Jenny cover her own mouth. Experience your blood filming down your cheeks. They say you are the only one injured.

Lay on the hot pavement in front of the truck. Realize you are still chewing your gum, while cars are still passing by. When James starts asking you questions about Bon Iver, notice the softness in his voice and know he is trying to keep you conscious. Chew the stale gum and answer all his questions. Talk about everything you know about Bon Iver. Cover your head with James's white dress shirt. Hear Jenny crying and gasping while she is standing above you with her cell phone. Understand you have a gash. Say something weird, like you are still chewing your gum.

Love your life. Think about fighting.

Say you are conscious when a man appears. Say "thank you" when the man identifies he is a doctor, someone who had pulled over, dressed in civilian clothes. Say your name is "Richard" and call him "Brian." Say you are conscious when there are paramedics. Say you feel no pain in your legs when they ask. Look up at moving clouds when they massage you into a neck brace. Say you are conscious. This is the first time you have been inside an ambulance, so remember everything. Love your life. Feel convinced you have no regrets. Feel the ambulance drive away and the road beneath your back.

richard chiem was born in 1987 and currently lives in seattle. richard is the author of the story collection *you private person*. richard is heavily influenced by joy williams, dennis cooper, and clarice lispector. richard listens to "half right" by elliott smith a lot.

THIS IS HOW I WILL SELL MORE POETRY THAN ANY POET IN THE HISTORY OF THE POETRY

i am releasing a book in the shape of a pizza
i know what you're thinking
"it looks like a pizza"
well i have news for you
it is a pizza

santino
@santinodela

TODAY I AM GOING TO DO THE THINGS I LOVE WITHOUT SELF DOUBT OR FEAR OF JUDGMENT BECAUSE THIS IS MY LIFE

 santino
@santinodela

watch me change my life

 santino
@santinodela

I want to run away from the cops with u and I want to hide in a bush and be very quiet with u. I want to escape from the cops with u.

 santino
@santinodela

you had me at 'i wrote an ebook'

 santino
@santinodela

if you want to be great, just be it

 **santino**
@santinodela

only death will shut me up

 santino
@santinodela

i've had too much to think

 santino
@santinodela

practice makes perfect and nobody is perfect
so we keep practicing

santino dela was born in 1990 and currently lives in vancouver, canada. santino is the creator of the illhueminati, an open and ever-expanding community of people sharing their art and writing on twitter. santino's personal twitter, one of the most prolific in this book, sends out dozens of new poetic anthems and mantras each day.

LOOKS

LIKE

THE

CATS

out of the bag

thank you so much they don't belong there.

BE PRESENT

BECAUSE THE WORLD NEEDS YOU

brian ecklund was born in 1991 and currently lives in pennsylvania. a graphic designer, photographer, musician, and poem artist, brian has released several books of typographic poems, including *p(ohm) s volume 1* and *some poems in bodoni.*

43

pancho
@BornToChill

My favorite poetry is when you can just talk to a person for a long time because you want to

pancho
@BornToChill

Be real ... how much of peanut butter is straight up butter

pancho
@BornToChill

Read one of my poems to my roommate; he said "it's not Robert Frost but not bad"

pancho
@BornToChill

Cmon people, what are you doing. Humans, realize you are connected to every other life

pancho
@BornToChill

Feel like apologizing for every human in behalf of every human

pancho
@BornToChill

Don't wanna see things as 'art'. Just things that ppl do

pancho
@BornToChill

Imagine there is someone to come, in the future, that will get so many followers on twitter he is Jesus... think about it...

pancho
@BornToChill

What if... [somewhere to sit] was as important to humans as like... water, and everyone brought [seat] along with them everywhere they went

pancho
@BornToChill

What if I went to the movies with my blanket

pancho
@BornToChill

What if I straight up got married lol

pancho
@BornToChill

What drives a body to scroll endlessly

pancho
@BornToChill

Don't think of the future and don't remember the past. There is only one moment & it is always happening. This moment is unique & perpetual.

pancho
@BornToChill

Devote your entire being into whatever moment you are living.

pancho
@BornToChill

If you feel like a dog... that's good

pancho espinosa was born in 1991 and currently lives in santa cruz, california. he's released an e-book of his own poetry, and an ebook of sexts with mira gonzalez. he loves soccer, and he wants to tell everyone to start riding a bike instead of driving.

JOSHUA JENNIFER ESPINOZA

FROM *IF YOU DON'T THINK CRYING IS POETRY YOU CAN GO FUCK YOURSELF*

i had another panic attack on the freeway
it wasn't interesting and i didn't have anything to say about it really
except that it felt as though god was swinging his fists
at the air directly above me

i've noticed when i write about god with
an antagonistic slant
i tend to use male pronouns
and when i write about god as
something more subtle or even benevolent
i always use female pronouns

on a daily basis i find myself becoming
less and less concerned with other people's idea of what poetry is
and also with my own idea of what poetry is

i am like mark wahlberg in boogie nights
but instead of having a giant penis
i have a giant heart
and when it metaphorically unfurls out in front of me
i am sitting cross-legged on my bed
crying my eyes out
and whispering into my front-facing camera phone
'i am a star, i am a star, i am a big bright shining star'
and if you don't think that is poetry
you can go fuck yourself

i sat on the hard steps in january,
looking up your nose while you shouted
'nothing matters, nothing matters, can't
you see that it's all smog?'
and that's great, that's really great
i ate plain cornflakes for breakfast
every day like a goddamn dork
and you're fucking off every moment
like sugar was never invented
i guess these mountains must feel
nice inside all of this fog but i
just want to be dead in my backyard
with you standing over my body
and will be in two months,
it'll be snowing and i'll be staring
up at the stars screaming from behind
my eyelids about how everything
is too much this or too much that
and maybe when you're gone
i'll queer myself back up and throw out
all those ugly flannel shirts you liked
to wrap around my little arms
i don't care, i don't care, can't you see
that we were all just clouds
the sun forgot to ruin?

FROM *I HAD A DREAM ABOUT THE END OF THE WORLD AND YOU WEREN'T IN IT*

i hear the orange sound of a trumpet
parting the clouds
late at night

where are you

you are the sound the moon makes
when it is tired of being used
as a romantic object

FROM *SYNESTHESIA*

i wanted to be dead
so i drew a picture of an owl
and left it on god's doorstep
but she was too kind
too wrapped up in her sunny
disposition to grant my wish

she kissed me on the cheek

she wrapped flowers around my head

she turned me into a pretty girl

i fell in love with god
and i was happy
but still wished i was dead

i wanted to be with god
in queer heaven forever

joshua jennifer espinoza was born in 1987 and currently lives in riverside, california. the author of several ebooks, she is passionate about challenging norms and cultivating more power and visibility for trans people, queers, and women. her writing lives at the intersection of distress over the state of the world and overwhelming love for the beauty that surrounds us every day.

U ARE LIKE AN OAT TO ME I LOVE U

when im with u i get that thrill of deleting over 40 unread emails off
my phone one after another

u are a young and very nocturnal animal stretching out on grass in a
way that makes me love u or else u are
two scalene triangles pushed together to form a stylized lightning
bolt for me

i often think that
the way the lights line the night-heavy walkway is not enough
i feel cold wanting sand pushed in me by ur wheat-blown hands

sometimes i fantasize about placing ur hand on a patch of soil in
such a way that bean sprouts that i previously planted in the soil
would sprout up between ur fingers
does this seem
hot to u

u are the most genetically similar to a barn owl that a person could
get while still technically being human

there are parts of me that have trailed behind u in a toyota rav 4
picking up small and curling petals that u have left behind u

when im with u i get that thrill of existing on a planet thats rotating
around and around a gigantic hot orb of fire

sometimes i fantasize about spray painting ur torso a soft pink color
while ur lying down with ur eyes shut and wearing a black shirt

yes
i want to drop
a cake on u

PASSION PROPELLER EROTIC INSTRUCTIONS: YOUR MAN LIES ON TOP OF YOU, ENTERING YOU IN TRADITIONAL MISSIONARY STYLE, BUT THEN — YOWZA! — HE STARTS DOING A 360-DEGREE SPIN, ALL THE WHILE KEEPING HIS PENIS DEEP INSIDE OF YOU. AS HE'S ROTATING AND THRUSTING, HELP GUIDE HIM AROUND YOUR BODY LIKE A PROPELLER WOULD SPIN AROUND THE TOP OF A HELICOPTER. MAKE SURE TO LIFT HIS LEGS WHEN THEY SWING AROUND OVER YOUR HEAD.

im trying to incorporate more parkour into my sex life. through a series of tests that i recently conducted in my small in-home laboratory, i learned that simply deciding that you want to photosynthesize doesn't automatically give you the ability to do it. (these controversial test results subsequently caused a huge rift within the scientific community as well as my personal life, but that's neither here nor there). im learning to interact more productively with the world in a number of ways. im learning to reap emotional reinforcement from reading the packaging of products.

life hack: boxes of cereal are often trying to tell you that you are good and that you deserve good things. you can read boxes of cereal to feel assured of this. boxes of cereal are also often trying to sell you cereal. this is not important, nor is it part of the life hack.

life hack: clouds exist. i dont know why. all i know is that my parent's met on a message board on neopets.com when they were 12 and 13 years old, respectively, and now im here.

the planet earth keeps continuously converting humanity into more and more babies. in the meantime im reading the wikipedia pages of artistic movements and dropping references to them more often in conversation with peers and superiors. my linkedin profile is simply a click-through link to my okcupid profile. its working really well for me, thanks. trying to discern whether or not your head is "an uncool size" is not productive, nor is it a life hack. drinking tea is a life hack, but only if you like tea. liking the idea of tea doesn't count.

i've become o.k. with the idea of robots rising up to destroy the way of life as we know it, but only because the way of life as we know it is such that it's very hard for humans to destroy it themselves.

life hack: speed up the settings of your life so you're experiencing it at 2 seconds per second; you'll be done in half the time.

life hack: pour kool aid in your wounds, why not?

life hack: doors can be used to enter one room from a different room.

life hack: disposing of pollutants in impoverished areas means less chance that a person living there will be financially capable of suing you if said pollutants seriously harm their health and the health of their loves ones.

life hack: clouds exist.

minnesota mom improves her quality of life with this ONE WEIRD TIP: acknowledging the fleeting nature of existence and resolving to be nice to and help others.

its important to decide to do things only after already confirming that you have the ability to do them. however, i still haven't given up on photosynthesizing.

word document
@weird_bug

feelin like global warming rn in the sense that i am incredibly hot yet the human race as a whole is not addressing me meaningfully

word document
@weird_bug

honestly suspected my sudden need to pee as the result of someone far away outsourcing their pee to me, just now, half-asleep

word document
@weird_bug

humans are basicly just really smart plants

word document
@weird_bug

clifford the big red dog was a GMO

word document
@weird_bug

seems crazy that bill cosby could be anywhere ..... like truly i have no clue where he is ...

55

word document
@weird_bug

halfway to consciousness this morning, felt afraid i had been sleeping in a way that had been reinforcing capitalism

word document
@weird_bug

feel uncomfortable w/ ~60% of instances where a man/men mentions/discusses a woman/women

word document
@weird_bug

thought "im high on birth control" for no reason

word document
@weird_bug

i spilled ramen broth in my bed & kind of don't care... this is by no means rock bottom but still probably farther down than i want to be...

word document
@weird_bug

omg we get to do nice things for others on this earth what the hell thats so cool

word document
@weird_bug

how can i somehow...use selfies..to stop climate change...

word document
@weird_bug

i want 2 use my existence 2 b a threat 2 oppressive systems

word document
@weird_bug

ronald reagan in a bane mask

word document
@weird_bug

an old man scrolling thru the instagram account he made as a teen w shaking fingers. "yolo..." he whispers, wiping a tear from his eye.

catalina gallagher was born in 1993 and currently lives in maine. catalina is a vegan and a student activist for climate justice and justice in palestine. coiner of the slogan "poop and cry in bed for three years," catalina literally wears a criss angel mindfreak t-shirt on a regular basis.

WELCOME TO YOUR
PAST   LIFE
UNFORTUNATELY YOU
ARE
A   VENTRILOQUIST

BEAUTY CAN BE FOUND IN ANYTHING, EVEN, MAYBE
ESPECIALLY, IN DESPERATION. WHEN I WANT TO STEP
IN FRONT OF A BUS I KNOW I AM BEAUTIFUL
BECAUSE THOSE MOMENTS ARE ACCOMPANIED BY
A MOMENTARY INTUITIONAL CONSCIOUSNESS OF
WHAT IT IS TO BE HUMAN AND A FUTILE LUST FOR THE
LACK OF IT. EVEN DESPERATION CAN BE BEAUTIFUL.
BEAUTY IS REAL AND YOU CAN FIND IT NEARLY
ANYWHERE; HOPE EXISTS AND I FIND IT MOST OFTEN
CURLED LIMP ON THE SIDE OF THE ROAD.

WE WILL ALL
EXPLOIT THE LAND
AND EACH OTHER
WE WILL DRY OUR
BLOOD ON THE SKIN
OF
EACH OTHER

IT IS A GREAT DAY IN
AMERICA
YOUR HAIR IS BEAUTIFUL
NOW WE BURN THE
LIBRARIES AND STORM
THE SUBURBS

WE DONT DESERVE
ANYTHING

WATCHMES LEEP & BREATHE POISON INTO MY HEART. I AM PREPARED TO SACRIFICE MYSELF TO ANYTHING. DIE EARLY; PROTECT YOURSELF FROM EVIL.

WAKE UP, I LOVE YOU. IMAGINE YOURSELF IN TWENTY YEARS, KISSING THE FEET OF ANY MACHINE, WHILE I CONSOLE YOU ABOUT THE ARMS OF WINTER. IT IS WARM HERE. LIE WITH ME.

IF YOU MAKE ART, YOU'D BETTER BE HELPING PEOPLE. THE WORLD HAS ENOUGH WASTE. THE PUENTE HILLS LANDFILL IS 500 FEET HIGH. YUCCA MOUNTAIN MAY SOON BE FILLED WITH SPENT NUCLEAR FUEL. AND YET, SOMEHOW, YOU ARE THE TORTURED ARTIST. "L'ART POUR L'ART" IS THE REFUGE OF COWARDS AND FASCISTS.

NOD YOUR HEAD TO SIGNAL THAT YOU AGREE WITH EVERYTHING ANYONE SAYS IN CASUAL CONVERSATION. MAKE THEM KNOW YOU ARE LIKABLE. DESTROY THEM FROM THE INSIDE.

A BRIEF JUSTIFICATION OF MY USE OF MACROS

recently someone told me that making macros doesn't make sense and that i should let my work 'stand on its own,' which i think is funny because that comment, from the start, is based on a privileging of words over images. why are words more important than images?

i make macros in an effort to attain some type of oneness with myself. that pursuit is necessary for me due to my diverging interests in art forms. i don't want to separate aspects of my life from one another. i don't see any value in separation. why should macros be seen as words on a background, instead of a home for words? the work is not the words, to me, but the effect produced by their combination with an image. the image is inextricable. the image is not a "background." "background" implies that the images are of lesser importance. my macros are fundamentally based on formal choices related to color, font, formatting, balance, and line that are designed to have as large of an impact on the perception of the work as the words themselves.

the "meaning" of every poem is determined in part by its surroundings. i will perceive the same poem differently based on whether it is printed on a blank white page, sprayed onto the side of a government building, or tattooed onto my friend's forearm. this is part of being an attentive reader. as such, to demean context as "background" does not fully account for the impact of paratextual elements.

macros are things in themselves, not servants of words. good literature is often ruined by the over-zealous love of words.

james ganas was born in 1993 and currently lives in seattle. he was the only author ever published (in e-book form) by lief books, the predecessor of boost house. he's a neo-marxist. he loves kanye west, art history, and game shows.

FROM A CONVERSATION AT A PARTY

you are all the different names for breasts / you are all the
unflushed toilets in the city of Chicago tonight / you walk into
the room and the temperature is raised three degrees / celsius
/ you, "light of my life, fire of my loins. My sin, my soul," are
the seagull chewing on a halffinished Big Mac in the Jewel-
Osco parking lot / you are the coke bust on the evening news
/ you are misery in the form of something beautiful, charming
in the way flowers on a grave are charming / you are banality
with clothes on / you are sentiments smushed together and
set before me / you're my Rushmore / you are a rush of blood
to the head by Coldplay / you are the band Coldplay / you are
Coldplay / you are your roommate's DVD copy of Failure to
Launch starring Matthew Mcconaughey and Sarah Jessica
Parker in her third feature film since the finale of Sex and the
City / you are the Fountain of Latona / you are the walls of
Jericho / you are Francois Truffaut / Surely you are the movie
Airplane / you are why the caged bird sings / you are the
symmetry of the sky upon the sea / you are the life story of
every person I've ever sat next to on a train / you are a pregnant
woman smoking cigarettes for shock value / you are the
moment when setting yourself on fire becomes passe / you are
the mist on the windshield when Scully sighs past Mulder's lips
/ you, sweet sunset of my soul, are six, no, five and a half jars
of nutella on my kitchen counter / "I wanna get lost in your rock
n roll and drift away" / you the dog's dried salivations on the
morning paper / you unending rain / you collapsing glacier / you
the fire that melts to make whole / "you got a face with a view"
/ you the older Chinese woman at the Bryn Mawr Starbucks
every night calling me a pretty boy and asking if i want her
sweets / you the guy who walks into the bookstore, sees
there's a poetry reading, then walks back out / you the potential

lover asking just exactly how old i am / you the potential lover adjusting your methods of interaction based on just exactly how old i am / you the scholar in the armchair / you the scholar on the couch in the bar adjacent to the movie theater / you the voice of art / you the fart in the crowded elevator / you interrogation of our cultural lexicon / you bent along the curved embankment of the Chicago Riverwalk / your hair browned from last summer's sun / is this you or a memory that haunts me? / you Rube Goldberg heart / you squashpics.com / you Antietam foot massage / you are the Red that matadors hold up to inflame such passions in the bull that it loses itself / and i like to imagine that the way i lose myself in you is tragic to some comparable proportion / *AHEM* "in this life, to die is not new / but to live, of course, is no newer" / TURN MY MIC UP / TURN UP MY MIC

PHONE CALL TO MOM

yeah mom, it's the same bank i go to
the one on berwyn over by that chinese
      restaurant we went to for your birthday two years ago
it's
it's yeah mom
it's like
yeah mom
yeah i remember that waiter with the
no mom listen i'm trying to
mom
mom
i'm trying to tell you about this bully
      bandit guy that robs that one bank i
paint? what? i
mom
no mom i never said anything about paint
i said bank
bang-k
no mom not
no not paint, bank

yeah i'll be careful
yeah mom i'll
mom
don't worry
there's nothing to worry about, if i
  or anyone has or discovers information
  they should call the FBI at (312) 421-6700

cean gamalinda was born in 1993 and currently lives in chicago. for two years he wrote a long poem in the form of a scroll, excerpted here—*a conversation at a party*. the full poem takes over two hours to read aloud. cean's writing engages an energetic exchange between pop culture and avant-garde poetics. cean has one parent instead of two, and the parent is soulja boy.

A QUESTION OF ETHICS,
A QUESTION OF MORALITY

Would you
let a Grinch
steal X-Mas
if he needed
it to feed his
starving fam-
ily????????

THE DAY THE GOVERNMENT
BANNED SEX

the day the government banned sex people were obviously
mad. everyone went outside and started smashing cars with
baseball bats and screaming. "the only reason i own a car
is so i can fuck inside of it!" yelled one woman. naturally, the
cars soon were lit on fire and people smashed storefront
windows out of blinding rage. when the storefront windows
were smashed, the tvs inside looked so perfectly stealable, so
everyone began to loot. the looting soon died down, though,
and was replaced by clandestine masturbation. everyone
furiously masturbated in alleyways and behind large trees and
shrubs. the police sent in to control the SexBan Riots (as they
would later be called) were unable to apprehend the crowd of
furious, clandestine masturbators because they were really well
hidden. the streets ran kind of clear kind of milky with semen
and that weird wet shit that comes out of vaginas.

the day the government banned sex all of the grown men cried. all of the grown men cried and took off their jackets and hats and put them down on the ground. "ee won't need these," they said. "we will never fuck again." all of the grown men cried and took off their dicks. "i didn't even know i could do that," said one man, holding his dick in his hand. we learn new things about our bodies every day. but who could even care about detachable dicks at a time like this?

the day the government banned sex two conventionally attractive people locked eyes from across a room, but there was no incentive for either to strike up conversation. "i just don't know why i would talk to a woman if i cannot legally have sex with her," the man would later tell his friends while they were taking baseball bats to the only remaining undamaged car on the street. the woman was shocked to find that she, too, didn't know why she would talk to women if sex was banned. in fact, after the great sex ban of 2013 (as it would later be called), no one ever spoke to a woman again.

the day the government banned sex all of the men and women in america bought teal gaucho pants. "i never once thought i would rock gauchos, but here i am," said one father of four. everyone agreed that gaucho pants were the best way to completely eradicate the public's sex drive. it took a couple of days for retailers to meet the high demand for these midcalf wonders, but the results—when everyone was finally outfitted— were astounding. "i don't want to fuck anyone now," said a woman, freely squatting in her teal gauchos.

the day the government banned sex everyone was really confused. "well what counts as sex?" they asked. congress was baffled. ohio senator rob portman jr. passionately filibustered on the issue for 69 hours as an ironic gesture and shout out to his old college frat buddies. "hilarious," said one of his boys back at dartmouth. but the issue remained perplexing! "can i at least touch someone's butt?" asked one woman. everyone agreed that touching someone's butt was sexy but not quite sex. the world breathed a collective sigh of relief.

VARIATIONS ON A THEME

2 Chainz
3 Chainz
4 Chainz
5 Chainz
6 Chainz
7 Chainz
8 Chainz

BITCH IM THE CENTRAL PARK HELLO KITTY

shut your oblique ass mouth im using this bagel bite as a telephone
dont tell me about the fucking weekend im already there
john candy burned down my barrel house
i was making that barrel house a home goddamnit
fuck you you lazy policemen get a job already
dont touch my fucking sanddollars
bitch im the central park hello kitty
i was raised in a moon bounce
my white gloves are fear
there is a nautical theme & i am in it
dont look now im using my 3G
bitch im the central park hello kitty
while you weren't looking i sprayed axe body spray on your car keys
pleasure is a town & i am taking U there
theodor adorno can suck my dick
im great w the kids
bitch im the central park hello kitty

cassandra gillig was born in 1993 and currently lives in new jersey. cassandra is a gluten-free vegan, recently honored as a resident in the 89plus exhibition in zürich, "poetry will be made by all!" cassandra has released a poetry album, sex beach, and wants to be buried in a casket that has a "coexist" bumper sticker on it. cassandra's grandmother has been making "gillig's island" jokes for years. the alphabetical order of this book's contributors was disrupted to honor cassandra's request to be next to her longtime friend and favorite poet, cean gamalinda.

HERE ARE SOME THINGS TO BE THANKFUL FOR

- shrek
- the emotional ability to feel empathy & appreciation
- shrek 2
- shrek the halls
- the shorts before pixar movies
- holy santos candles
- eating a sucker while in the shower
- the fact that your hand can make a turkey shape so you dont even have to be good at art and you can still decorate your house
- lil goats
- bread pudding
- bread of all shapes, sizes and colors
- hugging people when you see them for the first time in 4 months or more
- falling asleep whenever you want
- eating all the chips in the bag and not throwing up
- cotton candy
- the difference between "please" and "thank you"
- micro leaves
- mother willow
- holding hands when youre excited
- the beatles(i guess)
- free breath mints
- boys who are good at playing with hair

FROM "I LOVE HIM & I'M WHITE"

i only want coffee after 9pm and i only think of you every so
often but
when i do i
want 7777777 cups and i want to tell you
little facts
i think my life would be better if it ended
but i got to watch it like the
midnight premier of the deathly hallows pt II
     (the advantage of being yourself is
touching
      only what youuuuu can touch
and loving nothing else)
snowflakes cuddled up on my hair//red pop staining my voice,
this power couple reaches for the only laugh
i've immediately found attractive
and pulls their gravity towards answering
your accidental
phone call.

Amelia Gillis
if you dont masturbate to lion king you are f'd up

72

dude the glaciers are asking for it

amelia gillis was born in 1992 and currently lives in michigan. with angela shier (pg. 166), amelia co-edits the literary magazine *the mall*, which has published many writers from this book. amelia's personal philosophy and organizing principle in life is "i'm the best."

Dear Father

The red weather is laying its eggs in my torso The eggs of
amnesia The red weather is flexing its terrible gills

The red weather is running radio wire through the holes
in my cheeks & giving me a plastic jaw filled with soft
decaying language

My sockets are draining onto the heath of diseased signs

I need a non-sign state A state not lined with corpses I
feel the machine between my legs shift & bulge

Dear Mother

I bent mine eye-sleeves around "bad-willing I" to believe in your
act of milk-violence The horse of wooden laughter forms the
skin of my eye-sleeves You break open & insert hundreds of
other eyes I with thousand open legs expect

FROM A POEM IS A SKIN THAT RUPTURES

The ha ha albino sky is rotting like meat in the poem's throat.
Sink yr fingers in2 the creamo dreamo seal meat. Ensorcel
yrself 4-evah in loaves of hottie blubber.

The poem arranges suitable animals 4 yr maxi yum. Chew until
u r reeling around in yr blubs. Yr bones dripping out

▲

I am rubbing one out on the horny techno body of the poem. In the middle of the crime pageant. This is gross retail.

Everyone wants to engage in fancy looking. Yr eyes erupt into horns & u gore the language matrix. To cheerily participate in wound culture. This is what it means to write a poem.

The poem documents yr howling. When u became one of the "illegally disappeared." Yr fey squirting & other infantile abysmia.

A poem is a see-through membrane. A site of peculiar witchy media & yr eventual collapse. Rabbity bodies mid-flinch. An anti-body on a ferral mission. Hello. Hello. All u muffdivers & cockgobblers.

Poems are a trilling necrofantasia. Even above ground. Even in weak-eyed heaven.

▲

Please get yr eye out of my wanghole so I can proceed.

Please push yr eye so far into my wanghole that I fail. I need a collapse. Like a swan rotating on a spit. I crawl into yr lap. The horizon is burning behind us & draining into an iced-out pimp goblet. This goblet is the body of the poem.

To get drained into. By some paradisical baller. This is to write.

lara glenum currently lives in baton rouge, louisiana. lara teaches english at louisiana state university and is the author of four books of poetry, including *pop corpse* and *maximum gaga.* lara is also a co-editor of the feminist poetry anthology *gurlesque: the new grrly, grotesque, burlesque poetics.*

we looked up at the moon

i said, "now that's an!"

you said, "an what?" i didn't

say anything. we looked

at the moon.

I'M FAIRLY CERTAIN THERE'S A WORD FOR THIS

you know that feeling you
get when someone says
something and you don't
quite understand them, so you
say "what?", and
they repeat themselves, and you still
don't understand, and
after doing this three more
times, you just laugh and say something
like "oh, yeah,
for sure"? well anyway,
i like you.
do you want to play
mini-golf some time?

IT'S OKAY—LET'S BE COLD TOGETHER

sometimes the world feels too big
for one person's problems
this is neither comforting
nor distressing
sometimes it is a wonder
my head doesn't explode

anyone reading this
might have someone to kiss—
they should do that
without waiting

for everyone else
i am swallowing
a warm mouthful
of tim horton's mocha
and my leg
can't stop bouncing

it is a flood from the skies
outside
but we won't feel it
when we're dancing

philip gordon was born in 1989 and currently lives in british columbia, canada. he is a feminist who's passionate about ending kink-shaming and discrimination based on sexuality. he's a student in creative writing, and his favorite planet is saturn.

Tom hank

remeber there is good and bad in everthing

caesar was a bad guy but it is a gooood salad

cold sore is bad on your mouth but cold slaw is good inside of there

spinach is good bu t the spinach inquisition was so bad

(these examples are food but its true for other things to)

so be carful we only have one life together and it is sometimes very complicate d

give someone a brake today
they are doing there best i promise

have a grate dang day
im tom

Tom hank

face it where theres a wilson theres a way

have a grate day im tom hank

Tom hank

seems like bats are coll but have lots of secrets

Tom hank

do u ever think to yourslef----

wow im tom hank will i ever be abel to stop colecting these cats or will i just keep geting more and more cats until they overtake me im tom hank

anyway have a grate day

Tom hank

**today movie Trivia *

working title for "'catch me if you can" was "'ketchup in a can" but i said nobdy will beleive it because ketchap is in a botle

then get this i said "that title is not CATChy enough ! " and stephen spibler petted me on the head like a lovely animal and said "aw tom u maniac u did it againe "

i looked at his beautifull sun glasses and beard and you guesed it i thought: "nice '

so anyway as you know it is tuesday so why not just have a grate dang day

love your buddy tom hank :¬]

Tom hank

give me frogen yogurt or were going to have a problem

lol

just kiddein no problem here im tom

Tom hank

in my drem i was listening to my music (the 'best i ever had ' song by drale) and meg ryan was in the drem

meg said "i love your ear buds !'

and i said "wowe thank u yes they are my frends that are in my ears"

but i realized she was talking to a doge amd actualy she was saying "i love you air bud" and yup it turnt out the doge was air bud and i cryed one cute rose petal

but it was still a grate drem tho bc it had meg and air bud and drale and i was alive and im tom and you guessed it your alive to

have a grate wekend :]

Tom hank

isnt it weird how we can jus love as much as we want

wat a grate thing u have unlimited ability to show other people u love them and u can make them hapy jus by liveing

im listein to beyonce this mornin so im extra reved up nice

havea grate dang day im tom hank as ever

Tom hank

its like ever day u can either be nice or be meane

its hard to be ncie all the time but today lets be nice okay

nice have a grate day im tom hank

Tom hank

tom hank savety bulletin

im here to say one thing tonite

bob saget actualy is leonardon decapreo

have u ever watced family maters u cane see it in his smile......

watch again im tom hank

Tom hank

one coll thing bout the sun is that it come back for more every day even when thinges on this planet get very bad

remeber today that were all under the same sun

nice.

have a grate day im tom

tom hank
@TomHankThatsMe

rain looks sad but Its never sad

tom hank
@TomHankThatsMe

its ok u are all beatiful and u dont need to buy anyting to try to change jus try to be nice to every perspn you meet

tom hank
@TomHankThatsMe

yes its OK to be sad too we are all goin to die just like Wilson some day but at least we half each other

tom hank is a facebook page and twitter account that have been run anonymously since 2012. the accounts seem to have close ties with the characters matt romney and rob paul, who became popular during the 2012 u.s. presidential election, as well as the facebook page phil collin. using a profile picture of jim carrey instead of tom hanks, the posts often make puns referencing tom hanks movies while including heavy misspellings. accounts like tom hank and matt romney present interesting new possibilities for storytelling online, building fictional characters over time with small, regular social media updates.

MICHAEL HESSEL-MIAL

earth is dieing>>??
how the fk is tat possible??
earth+die..?? 0_0"

Dead Fish in Jersey Shore
Dead fish in Chesapeake Bay
Dead fish in Brazil
Dead Doves in Italy

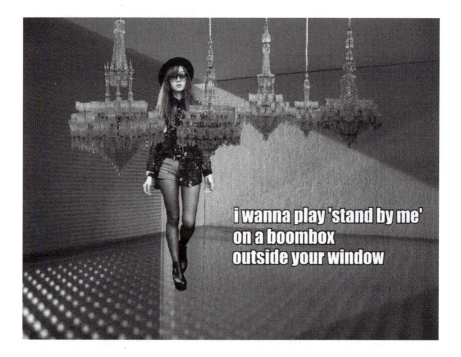

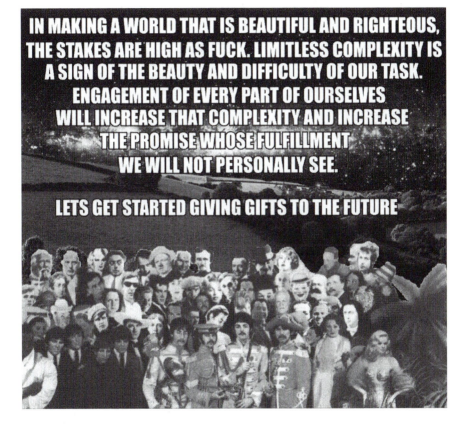

IN MAKING A WORLD THAT IS BEAUTIFUL AND RIGHTEOUS, THE STAKES ARE HIGH AS FUCK. LIMITLESS COMPLEXITY IS A SIGN OF THE BEAUTY AND DIFFICULTY OF OUR TASK. ENGAGEMENT OF EVERY PART OF OURSELVES WILL INCREASE THAT COMPLEXITY AND INCREASE THE PROMISE WHOSE FULFILLMENT WE WILL NOT PERSONALLY SEE.

LETS GET STARTED GIVING GIFTS TO THE FUTURE

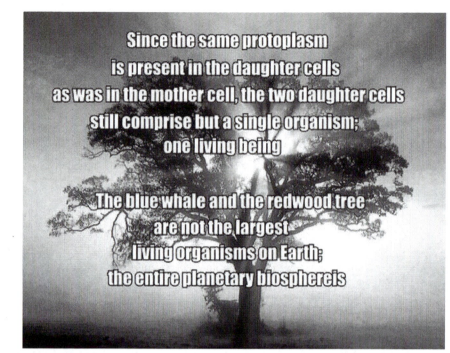

Since the same protoplasm
is present in the daughter cells
as was in the mother cell, the two daughter cells
still comprise but a single organism;
one living being

The blue whale and the redwood tree
are not the largest
living organisms on Earth;
the entire planetary biosphere is

 Michael Hessel-Mial
@mikehesselmial

ppl b like, "y u still makin macros in impact font mike?"

& i tell em

"moving mountains takes force, not acceleration"

#greatestpoetalive

Michael Hessel-Mial
@mikehesselmial

so many poetry books in my bed and none of them are you

Michael Hessel-Mial
@mikehesselmial

i said it once and i'll say it again - Become The Horse Ebooks Of Yourself

Michael Hessel-Mial
@mikehesselmial

Daily reminder that people hate Kanye because he threatens the stability of the structural racism they benefit from

Michael Hessel-Mial
@mikehesselmial

it blows me away that trying to make the system fairer & ecologically sustainable is seen as some crazy romantic dream - rather than a duty

michael hessel-mial was born in 1987 and currently lives in atlanta. michael runs the tumblr blog *internet poetry*, and has authored multiple e-books, including the image macro collection *mspaint and heartbreak*. michael is passionate about humans building symbiotic, sustainable relationships with the nonhuman world. a phd student in comparitive literature and cybernetics, michael is also a self-proclaimed "ukulele master" and the self-proclaimed "#greatestpoetalive."

87

Horse ebooks
@Horse_ebooks

Some people think French kissing is no big deal. It s just like a regular kiss, but with a little added tongue-action.

That s dead wrong.

Horse ebooks
@Horse_ebooks

Who Else Wants To Become A Golf Ball

Horse ebooks
@Horse_ebooks

Dear Reader,

You are reading

Horse ebooks
@Horse_ebooks

(using fingers to indicate triangular shape) SMELL SMELL SMELL GOOD NEW NEW NEW slice drink MATCH SPARKLER (thrown in air) STARS STARS STARS

Horse ebooks
@Horse_ebooks

stress me out and destroy my home

Horse ebooks
@Horse_ebooks

Don t worry if you are not computer

Horse ebooks
@Horse_ebooks

HOLY COW!!... DOG TOYS ARE GETTING EXPENSIVE WHY NOT

Horse ebooks
@Horse_ebooks

We re very lucky today

Horse ebooks
@Horse_ebooks

Bread Taco

Horse ebooks
@Horse_ebooks

GLIMPSE AT MY LIFESTYLE

Horse ebooks
@Horse_ebooks

Not only that, but whether you believe it (or want to believe it) the car salesmen will continue to laugh

Horse ebooks
@Horse_ebooks

Ask your dumbass friends if they know of a reputable artist.

Horse ebooks
@Horse_ebooks

What the Aztec

Horse ebooks
@Horse_ebooks

Are you ready to have a swan?

Horse ebooks
@Horse_ebooks

ORONGLY DGAGREE DISAGREE NO G G NO G G G G G G G NO G G NEIEHER AGREE NOR DGAGREE O O O no O O no O O no O O no neither neither neither

Horse ebooks
@Horse_ebooks

ANYONE Increase Their Height All You Need

Horse ebooks
@Horse_ebooks

YOU ARE ABOUT TO DISCOVER LIFE
CHANGING INFORMATION!

Horse ebooks
@Horse_ebooks

Imagine growing a flower

Horse ebooks
@Horse_ebooks

Well I ve got a heap of yummy recipes that
are completely gluten

Horse ebooks
@Horse_ebooks

As you might know, I am a full time Internet

Horse ebooks
@Horse_ebooks

I am the Money King - And the good news is
that I AM A MILLIONAIRE

Horse ebooks
@Horse_ebooks

Their negativity only served to push me deeper into the realms of soap making.

Horse ebooks
@Horse_ebooks

it was absolutely useless. Thanks

@horse_ebooks was a twitter spambot created in 2010 by russian web developer alexey kouznetsov to sell e-books. the bot gained a small cult following for its hilarious tweets before being taken over by artist **jacob bakkila** in september 2011. the account grew quickly in popularity as bakkila worked in secret, performing as a spambot for two years, finally ending the project in 2013 with over 200,000 followers. the original context of all lines tweeted by @horse_ebooks can be found by searching them in quotes, as bakkila used a process similar to flarf poets such as sharon mesmer (p. 123) and k. silem mohammad (p. 131), ripping found text from previously written sources. bakkila also inserted a narrative throughout the tweets regarding a character named dalton, which tied into a follow-up project, bear stearns bravo. a rich subject for discussion on many fronts, @horse_ebooks has been a major influence on many writers in this book, and will likely be at the center of conversations about literature and the internet for decades to come.

WHAT IT LOOKS LIKE MY SPANISH SHIRT WASHING DIRECTIONS ARE SAYING TO ME

Instructions for shirt:

Don't remove.
Don't wash it second.

Wash with similar colors.

Wash this tomorrow or today, with frigid water (30°C) for shirt of
    your dreams.
With ham detergent.

Don't sleep with Chad!

Move to Colorado.

Remain sober.

Grow plants in medium temperatures (150°C) for shirt of your dreams.

Tela National.
Not responsible for additional processes.

DECEMBER 21ST, 2002

It's said it takes seven years to grow
completely new skin cells.
To think, this year I will grow
into a body you never will
have touched.

OH NO EVERYTHING

Oh no the stuff we're made of.
The blood and warmth
that attracts parasites,

the organs that swell with sickness,
the bodies that turn
inward to eat themselves.

Oh no dark corners and the men
who wait in them.

Oh no fire, oh no damp matches.
Oh no little ears that fill
with their parents' cusses.

Oh no the moon, grinning icy
and merciless over our dying
house plants.

Oh no the birds are leaving us now.
The leaves turning
to rot, and the boots
packing down the dead grass.

Oh no bears and sharks
and lust and anything else
that could devour us in a single second.

Oh no God.

Oh no
no God.

brett elizabeth jenkins was born in 1986 and currently lives in saint paul, minnesota. her two favorite words are "espionage" and "gubernatorial." brett is the poetry editor at *specter: a magazine of literature & art.*

POETRY

POETRY IS NOT PUBLISHED IN A BOOK
OR SCRIBBLED IN A JOURNAL.

IT IS NOT COMPOSED OF STRICT METER AND RHYME,
STANZA AND STRUCTURE,
ASSONANCE AND ALLITERATION.

POETRY IS NATURE.

POETRY IS NON-SEQUITUR.

POETRY IS THE WAY OUR HIPS AND LIPS
INTERTWINE LIKE GRASPING VINES
WITH DETERMINATION AND GRACE
THAT IS SIMPLY DIVINE.

POETRY IS THE WAY YOU WAKE UP ON A LAZY SUMMER
    SUNDAY MORNING
AND LISTEN TO THE HEARTBEAT OF YOUR LOVER
LYING NOT TOO FAR AWAY.

POETRY IS THE COMPASSION AND SELFLESS DESIRE
THAT CAUSES US TO BUY MEALS FOR STRANGERS
AND TIP EXTRA JUST FOR THE HELL OF IT.

POETRY IS THE FACT THAT EACH AND EVERY ONE OF US
IS ANOTHER INFINITELY RANDOM MANIFESTATION OF THE
UNIVERSE ATTEMPTING TO UNDERSTAND ITSELF THROUGH
CONVOLUTED COSMIC INTROSPECTION.

POETRY IS THE WAY THAT THE STARDUST FLOWS
THROUGH OUR VEINS AND THE LIMITLESS POTENTIAL OF
HUMAN CREATIVITY HIDES JUST OUT OF SIGHT BEHIND
OUR EYES.

POETRY IS THE WAY THE WISE WINDS BLOW SOFTLY
THROUGH THE TREES, WHISPERING SECRETS TO ANYONE
WHO WISHES TO HEAR.

POETRY IS THE WAY THE RIVER LOVINGLY EMBRACES
EACH AND EVERY PEBBLE IN THE RIVERBED LIKE A
MOTHER HOLDING HER NEWBORN SONS.

POETRY IS ORGANIC.
MALLEABLE.
THESE WORDS ARE NOT POETRY -
LIFE IS POETRY.
DEATH IS POETRY.
LOVE -
LOSS -
STRIFE -
SUCCESS -
POETRY.
WE ARE POETRY.

FROM STATE OF THE UNION ADDRESS

news flash: the illuminati and the reptilian overlords are not
trying to control your mind.

this is not about pineal gland calcification and third eyes but
about the systematic disenfranchisement and subjugation of
every man woman and child in this unfortunate nation.

they impose harsh sentences on small time drug crimes and
outsource our only sources of economic stability.
left with no upward mobility, we then resort to any means
necessary to simply survive.

'the world is your oyster.' they say. and they conveniently fail to
mention the fine print which emphatically states that you may
only possess the oyster shucking knife if you are white, male,
and upper middle class.

this is not about checking privilege and white guilt. this is about the way that this fucked up world works. about the sinister cogs turning behind the scenes.

and if you dare raise your voice in resistance you'll find yourself staring at cinderblock walls, spools of barbed wire, reinforced steel bars, and armed guards for the rest of your sad life. your enclosed inmate existence making the coffers of the prison-industrial complex even deeper.

some say we should raise our fists instead and fight. and i say to them good luck fight the world's most technologically advanced military in its own home territory. Guerilla warfare and armed millitias stand about as good of a chance as gorillas armed with sticks and stones when the enemy possesses satellites that can see your face from orbit.

and i hope you don't mind being despised by the public of the modern world when you're slapped in the face with that dreadful catch-all term that is 'terrorist'.

but we can't just sit here and let the vines of greed asphyxiate our vitality away.

so herein lies the eternal question that i pose to you:

what are we to do?

jon snow
@blaxstronaut

there is something to be said about the quality of our reality if we are constantly seeking mind-altering substances to escape it.

97

jon snow
@blaxstronaut

congratulations if you got out of bed this morning. that was a victory, and it takes a hundred little victories to win a war.

jon snow
@blaxstronaut

what if instead of being mean in peoples asks we were aggressively nice? "GOD DAMMIT I HOPE YOU LIVE A LONG LIFE FULL OF LOVE AND HAPPINESS"

jon snow
@blaxstronaut

HOLY SHIT I HOPE YOU FIND LOVE ONE DAY AND HAVE A BEAUTIFUL FAMILY

jon snow
@blaxstronaut

SMASH YOUR SCALES AND BREAK YOUR MIRRORS BECAUSE WEIGHT IS JUST A NUMBER AND BEAUTY DOES NOT DEFINE YOU #AGGRESSIVEPOSITIVITY

raymond johnson was born in 1994 and currently lives in baltimore. raymond's writing is nformed by his passionate political views regarding the prison-industrial complex, the millitary-industrial complex, american imperialism, racism, and social justice. in 2013 he started the "#AGGRESSIVEPOSITIVITY" hashtag on twitter, which has spread and gained wider popularity since.

Kenji Khozoei
@mfkenji

wow what a wonderful day to continue to approach my inevitable death

 Kenji Khozoei
@mfkenji

just imagine yelling 'nice wig, asshole' at a stranger

 Kenji Khozoei
@mfkenji

i just want to make the world hurt a little less because i was here

 **Kenji Khozoei**
@mfkenji

i'm so tired of not saying the things that i want to say, i'm so tired of not being the person that i want to be

Kenji Khozoei
@mfkenji

concentration of media ownership that's that shit i don't like

Kenji Khozoei
@mfkenji

societal reinforcement of conservative gender roles that's that shit i don't like

Kenji Khozoei
@mfkenji

western imperialism that's that shit i don't like

Kenji Khozoei
@mfkenji

can we all just stop and take a moment to realize that yolo isn't a joke

Kenji Khozoei
@mfkenji

it's time to get excited about using art to change the world for the better

Kenji Khozoei
@mfkenji

bro do u even appreciate salad

Kenji Khozoei
@mfkenji

well fk im sorry if my passion fr improving myself & the world is too much i can tone it down lol jk i love u have u looked at the sky recen

Kenji Khozoei
@mfkenji

do whatever makes you love you more

Kenji Khozoei

did you see the sky today? i was sitting in the lunch room at work looking out of the window and thinking about the phrase 'extreme weather conditions'. extreme. it's the middle of spring and the world is finally ending, thank god. did you know that some people still think rape jokes are funny? 'feminism' is the new f-word, ha ha. nice one. idiot. let's all hold hands and deny climate change together. let's yell at each other until the cows literally do come home. did you know that i stopped eating meat? some people get immediately defensive when i tell them that. sorry but i really didn't mean to remind you of your internalized guilt, rofl, #startedfromthebottom. don't worry about it. it'll make sense tomorrow, probably. imagine when the world is actually ending how fucking awesome is the sky gonna look then.

kenji khozoei was born in 1994 and currently lives in sydney, australia. kenji's work is strongly informed by his belief that "we have the opportunity today more than ever, as young people on the internet, to create an alternative way of thinking and living, if not for ourselves and each other then at least for whoever and whatever might be here after us." his influences include the internet, the sky, popular rap music, and the inevitable collapse of western civilization. for his birthday, kenji wants the relatively painless fall of capitalist society.

YOU CAN'T HANDLE MY BLOODHOLE

Imma manhandle my fatbags like a boss
Imma boorish catcall your funsacks like a man
the bags under my eyes are the death nuggets
combo w/ my age-defying eye cream-brulee
& they're harder than the bricks you shat in my purse during our
    movie night and just for that
Imma torch your house; lit with your beeswax
Imma rugburn your place down; like a boss on the secretary desk
Mind your own baloney business
& Go make me my balcony suicide sandwich

IMMA BLOODHOLE MY SINHOLE
GO SOUTH GO SOUR C'MON BOY C'MON SON
C'MON WEALTH C'MON POOR
C'MON MY MONGREL GOO OF THE GRUEL THAT WENT SOUR

IMMA BLOODHOLE MY SINHOLE
GO SOUTH GO SOUR COME GET IT BOY COME GET IT SON
GO DOWN ON ME GO DOWN TOWN ON ME
GO DOWN ON MY BLOODHOLE; THAT'S WHERE THE SHIT
   GOES DOWN

GO DOWNTOWN GET THE TEST DONE
GO DOWN GET THE SHIT DONE
BLOW THE POPSICLESTAND UP & TASTE THE RAINBOW

ji yoon lee is the author of the poetry chapbooks *imma* and
funsize/bitesize, as well as a full-length poetry collection,
foreigner's folly: a tale of attempted project. ji yoon has worked at
action books and taught creative writing at university of notre dame.

BOOK REVIEWERS ALWAYS PRAISE BOOKS AS 'LIFE-AFFIRMING' BECAUSE THE MORE HUMANS THERE ARE ON EARTH THE BETTER

i click a link on the internet
i watch a video
a bullfighter in spain
pushes a sword into a bull's shoulder
the entire sword goes down into the bull
like a toothpick into a plum

and the bull keeps moving and bucking
and as it moves around
the sword cuts up its insides
and i want to see the bull's eyes
but the video is quicktime
and the size of a baby's forehead cut in half
and i turn my head
to a different angle
so that i might see the bull's eyes
but this is on a computer screen
and two-dimensional
and now the bullfighter is cutting off the bull's ears
from behind, and the bull is on the ground, and shivering
as if it were cold, and just wanted a blanket, and a bed
and i deleted this line
and i deleted this line, too, in revisions
and i deleted this line that was talking about god
and this line was also talking about god and it said something
about the universe and i deleted it
and this line kept talking about semantics and i deleted it

LISA JARNOT

For some reason the Universe begins. Subatomic Particles move around. There are Atoms. The Atoms move around. Single-Cell Organisms are created. Fish are created. Lisa Jarnot is created. Lisa Jarnot sits at a computer. She has just completed a poem with rhyming structure AA BB CC DD EE. Lisa Jarnot stands, puts on a ski-mask, goes to the kitchen, places a Steak Knife in her purse. Lisa Jarnot walks outside. It is sunny. Lisa Jarnot walks quietly into a field. There is a motorcycle. Lisa Jarnot rides the motorcycle for forty minutes. "War-mongering George W. Bush," thinks Lisa Jarnot. Ahead is a river. Lisa Jarnot slows the motorcycle then leaps from it. She stumbles a little on the grass. The motorcycle goes into the river. Lisa Jarnot takes the knife from her purse. She walks toward a street. George W. Bush, one hundred feet away, is jogging on the street. Lisa Jarnot kneels behind a shrub. George W. Bush is forty feet away. Thirty feet. Twenty. Lisa Jarnot stands, runs at George W. Bush with the knife. George W. Bush blocks Lisa Jarnot's Steak Knife with his forearm. Lisa Jarnot falls, stands. George W. Bush's head is turned, he is screaming. Lisa Jarnot stabs George W. Bush thirty-five times. Thirty-two of the stabs occur after George W. Bush has fallen to the ground. A sniper shoots Lisa Jarnot in the head three times. Lisa Jarnot's corpse is taken away. Lisa Jarnot's skeleton lies in a coffin. George W. Bush's skeleton lies in a coffin. The sniper's skeleton lies in a coffin. The Steak Knife lies in a plastic baggy in a drawer. The Earth moves around the Sun at 67,000 miles per hour. The Solar System moves through the Milky Way at 100 miles per second. The Milky Way is a Galaxy. There are 35 Galaxies in the Local Group, which is a part of the Virago Supercluster. Scientists believe there are more than 10 million Superclusters in the Universe. No one knows where you go when you die. No one knows what consciousness is. No one knows why we are here. Etc.

Tao Lin
@tao_lin

1st line of my vampire novel: 'i couldn't remember if my age was ~10,000, ~100,000, or ~100,000,000 & i didn't care'

Tao Lin
@tao_lin

website called 'physically strongest writers'

Tao Lin
@tao_lin

memoir titled 'fucking insane'

Tao Lin
@tao_lin

Ted talk 'I Can Draw Anything' in which I continuously, openly lie about how I can draw absolutely anything (but in a convincing manner)

Tao Lin
@tao_lin

imagine someone w zero self-control, wld they just die within hours, or a few days, or something? seems funny

I FELT HAPPY WITHOUT DRINKING COFFEE TODAY

i looked at a girl and thought 'would i date her'
and thought 'yes' and felt happy and surprised
then i thought about girls i wouldn't date and felt nervous
then i looked at a girl and thought 'no, i wouldn't date her'
and felt happy again and not nervous anymore
i also felt happy after thinking 'ramen' at one point today

BIG MACS

i opened my kombucha
it tasted like big macs
that hasn't happened before
i thought about how i felt
i think i felt really bad

tao lin was born in 1983 and currently lives in new york city.
tao has published seven books since 2006 (and more e-books),
published other writers via the small press muumuu house, and
released films as mdmafilms. tao has been a major influence
for many younger writers in this anthology, a vital pillar of the
community that has become known as "alt lit."

hey,
we *are* alive.
maybe that's enough.

cayla lockwood is currently living in syracuse, new york. cayla makes a variety of text-based installations and artworks. an mfa student in printmaking and a fan of the show *rosanne*, cayla has been published by many of the central "alt lit" magazines and blogs. cayla owns a blue scarf with the facebook logo on it.

Patricia Lockwood
@TriciaLockwood

ALTERNATE THEORIES ABOUT ROBIN HOOD

1. He loved to fuck the trees
2. He got it on with trees
3. ?
4. ?
5. ??
6. Tree-fucker

Patricia Lockwood
@TriciaLockwood

Petition to change the word "husband" to "male wife"

Patricia Lockwood
@TriciaLockwood

I saw a bottle of dish soap in the shower & asked my mom what it was for & she looked at me & said "Your dad washes himself with dish soap"

Patricia Lockwood
@TriciaLockwood

Is there a sex position called babystyle? I
don't think there should be but I was just
wondering

Patricia Lockwood
@TriciaLockwood

Can't believe the second track on Yeezus
samples "the sound of a baby elephant giving
herself a bath"

Patricia Lockwood
@TriciaLockwood

Can't believe the third track on Yeezus is a
diss track for Hunt's Ketchup, "impostor
ketchup, which trembles in the shadow of
Heinz"

Patricia Lockwood
@TriciaLockwood

Can't believe the tasty beat on the sixth track
of Yeezus -- is the heartbeat of Kanye's
unborn child

Patricia Lockwood
@TriciaLockwood

I'm selling my body on Craigslist -- not for sex, but because it's haunted

Patricia Lockwood
@TriciaLockwood

Someone asked "what are some good words to describe chocolate" on Yahoo! Answers and half the people just responded "brown"

Patricia Lockwood
@TriciaLockwood

Sext: An iceberg whispers to you, "Just the tip"

Patricia Lockwood
@TriciaLockwood

Sext: I give you some medicine made out of tiger's penis. I'm a tiger. It's my penis. The ... the medicine is me having sex with you

Patricia Lockwood
@TriciaLockwood

So exactly how tiny IS this tim

Patricia Lockwood
@TriciaLockwood

"Stop giving away your content for free," my mom sobs on the phone. "No one will ever marry you if you give away your content for free"

Patricia Lockwood
@TriciaLockwood

Sex Sent Me To The ER: When I Realized What Sex Actually Was I Freaked Out So Much That I Lost It And An Ambulance Had To Take Me To The ER

Patricia Lockwood
@TriciaLockwood

You know that Eeyore kept losing that tail on purpose because he LOVED to get it nailed back on

Patricia Lockwood
@TriciaLockwood

Sex with Tigger would be so fucked up

Patricia Lockwood
@TriciaLockwood

Pretzel is just a breadstick that have tried to suck its own dick

114

Patricia Lockwood
@TriciaLockwood

Dear God take the power of speech from Ryan Gosling and allow him to communicate only in car sounds

Patricia Lockwood
@TriciaLockwood

I want to feel about anything the way dogs feel about Outside

Patricia Lockwood
@TriciaLockwood

Why write a book when you can just go into the woods and let your smell be information for the wolves

Patricia Lockwood
@TriciaLockwood

When my life flashes before my eyes I hope I get to see a lot of webpages

patricia lockwood was born in 1982 and currently lives in lawrence, kansas. crowned "poet laureate of twitter" by *htmlgiant*, patricia is widely known for her association with "weird twitter" as well as for her creation of the "sext" form on twitter. her poem "rape joke" was featured on *the awl* in july 2013, and quickly went viral, prompting a worldwide discussion on the culture of victim-blaming and rape jokes both within the poetry realm and beyond.

SCATTERSTATE

i am translation of warehouse. the maim cattle are fat envelope shapes. all envelopes are warehouse too. a different way to the same heavies brought a tangled shudder to big builds. any partner skin i encounter is syllable full, wordwater. you're right, i can be funny wet. my sides are brokens glancing up, one knucklebone in a burst hoof. i draw a little animal on our foreheads. the color is wearing juice, but why outloud them to myself? this is hard to draw from memory. this is heal too hard. this doesn't look like a cow at all. i can't go on. there are lines, there are darker trees that are the right height to sleep next to me. i can't, but i goon. my letter is titled, "crashmelt," and it reads like a whole shaved thing. one day was so bright and wearing hospital scrubs. i was opening a bottle on the street to taste it. a bit of bird carbonation went on about being punished with straps, mumbling tumors, mercy. all the ways they've told you to cheap your food down are cow shit. you've got a heart to keep awake. you can turn up the volume, but the static hasn't attached itself yet. it becomes a flock on the way out. i open my mouth. "all metal with the dump glowing," you say, looking in. i think i still see the envelopes i've sent around. there's one spilling lunch. i taste them when fluorescence is chewed at a party close to me. i see them around, looking for the thin crust shifts of my jaw but just barely where. "maybe you have something," you say, looking in. what's tilting back is the first south facing layer of the year. the first without coat of the creatures. parts were gone because our dry didn't punctuate. i am a little vile left and it gives me a part, a jar. i come at the pasture through short cuts. "maybe i do," i say. this portion thinks that lines are going through unearthing love all the time. does that convince you of something nice and used cup about me? that something buried alive is under my neckline? turns out it is just a different person with cloth cuts like mine. we splotched can be a similar low did person, a blow did person.

come learn how to grab a few before slamming it shut quick and going back out to the front of the house. what is swinging from your drop? you left it open and now you are hauling wane, even by its joints, inside my cheek. muscle clouds float by. i have completely taken lawns to get back to you i know. it's just that the envelope looks like muscle clouds to me sometimes. against it, it looks like we're hard at pushing. it can get all thin mall seams for us. i build out, get my brightness sore. i just mouthed fuck all the way down the page. that's a large mouth, population: cows. "split as split, jaw as stone," i said in my warehouse made out to blank. sorry, i popped out for a minute. so much is coming to me. we were standing with our sides out, shaking our lock moves. terror rhythm, are you still okay if i kiss it noise as i want? when your mouth is sad, make it the sweat lodge out there. make it slam ache ruts while the loving heads are dripping back. a few sounds will creep up like a picture sliding and knucking bone, a few sounds like functioning insides being needing come out swinging holes. then it'll be fine. it'll be fine and the softest jumbotron close up on your very good group of landscrape will flash across whatever surface. little flaps, they are having a moment that will mean carrying so much to us.

carrie lorig was born in 1986 and currently lives in minneapolis, minnesota. carrie is the author of the chapbook *nods*, and co-author of chapbooks with russ woods and nick sturm. a poetry editor for *coconut magazine*, carrie has described a sunset as "a chili pepper inside a blonde woman's mouth."

THE TERRIFYING TRUTH ABOUT GOD BEING DEAD IS THE FACT THAT FRANKENSTEIN WON'T CARE AND IF GIVEN THE CHANCE WILL ALMOST DEFINITELY BRING SOME PART OF HIM BACK

it does not feel surprising to me that the earth is getting bigger on the inside and no one thought to tell me this for two decades in passing or even books

or that darwin once deduced that plants are simple animals with their heads inside the ground and that's the reason their genitalia are so all up in our faces n'stuff

look at me i'm more you than you will ever be but don't feel surprised baby it'll ruin this moment of clarity for us both

i've decided to pursue becoming the most visible thing but a reality i have to grapple with is that the sun has set the bar very high

most things can live beside each other their whole lives never touching or recognizing they're the exact same thing and i find this deeply troubling

on a psychic level, i mean

i'm ripping off all poets when i tell you i love you and mean it and do mean it but then fail to love you in any specific way while knowing exactly why this happened

and am injuring my sense of self just by having heard of sense of self i think i love you and i mean it there i said it i'm sorry what's next

the funny thing about a hall of mirrors is that you can still call it
that when no one's inside but some people would argue there can
be no mirrors without people or some species of magpie looking
into them

i've spent time in the flesh-tempered depths of desensitization
and have just let my brain sit there for as long as i could stay
conscious and i see why people would want to not do this
because it's hell but hey hell's not so bad i recommend it

the ideas of precision distribution and distinction don't work very
well from a distance

you can ask any scientist and they'll argue with you about it for
one decade at least

the terrifying truth about war is that every argument can be
reduced to a pizza metaphor and that every pizza can be
modified to suit the purpose of helping your brain manifest more
and hopefully cheaper pizza as soon as humanly possible

i'm stealing these ideas and the way that i arrange them because
if i didn't someone else would and i have the luxury of knowing i
steal and arrange ideas better than anyone on earth

you're my favorite thing i've seen so far kiss me get it over with

if first google then facebook then candy crush then xkeyscore
then germany all became one thing i'd never mention nazis or the
holocaust again

while i'm being sensitive i guess i'll go ahead and blame the
tsunami in japan for september eleventh and see if that does
anything for you

love is a thing on sale for more money than there existed until
i insufflated half this line of granulated marble i chipped off
michelangelo's the david last week

dogmatic circumstance look at that a non sequitur

my grandma is seventy-five and then my father is fifty and then
again here i am i'm twenty-five and i honestly don't care about
anything except observations like these i've made

the truly awesome and therefore terrifying thing about the state of
the union is that i've never known what it meant

but it combined all ethnicities into one specific person after only a
million years of trying and came up with stephen michael mcdowell

did we do a good job they ask you demurely yes or no or maybe
kind of please share with friends plus one and retweet

❀*₀.ᐧ *∨ ("๑_๑)/*₀.ᐧ *❀
@stephenunedited

wow humans are shitty to themselves and
each other all over the world and have been
for ages ! who knew !! come hug me ! who'r
we to judge !

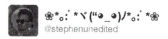
❀*₀.ᐧ *∨ ("๑_๑)/*₀.ᐧ *❀
@stephenunedited

just 'blacked in' from a baby carrot blackout,
half the bag gone, no memory of eating them,
frantically put bag in fridge/left kitchen

❀*₀.ᐧ *∨ ("๑_๑)/*₀.ᐧ *❀
@stephenunedited

hope drake finds what he's looking for in life

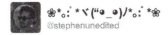
❀*₀:˙ *↖("๑_๑)/*₀:˙ *❀
@stephenunedited

i'm living proof that some pretty chill shit can
be derived from an arbitrarily assembled
clusterfuck of extremely unchill shit

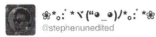
❀*₀:˙ *↖("๑_๑)/*₀:˙ *❀
@stephenunedited

seems insane to me that ppl do other things
like watch netflix instead of meditating... like...
there's an entire universe behind ur eyes...

**REGGAETON
MY NEMESIS
WE MEET AGAIN**

121

I'M COMPLETELY DISSATISFIED
WITH THE NUMBER OF CRICKETS
ON MY DICK

NONE (THERE SHOULD BE
THOUSANDS)

IN THE FUTURE THERE WILL BE
SIGNIFICANTLY MORE DEAD
PEOPLE

I AM SO HAPPY I HAVE NOT
THOUGHT THE WORD
'ENGORGED' TODAY

I KEEP FORGETTING AND
BEHAVING AS THOUGH LYNXES
DON'T EXIST

BUT THEY DON'T CARE AND JUST
KEEP LYNXING AROUND

I MISS THE INNUMERABLE
INSECTS OF YOU

stephen michael mcdowell (buttercup) was born in 1988 and currently lives in maryland. he is passionate about disabling systems of control, encouraging people to deprogram alienating and violent behaviors in themselves, and promoting the idea that "u r what u h8." stephen is the founder of habitat publishing and the author of *AN OPEN LETTER TO THOSE WHO HAVE ATTEMPTED TO FUCK WITH MY MOTHERFUCKING CLIQUE* among many other titles.

I AM SO INTO MY MOM

Mom, you can't play with my balls in Sheep Meadow anymore.
The signs say so, and so does that one uppity-assed white bitch.
Mom, I am now your infant overlord;
surrender now or I'll poop in your lap.
Mom, there is no word to describe your perfection.
Wait – are you dead?
I am so confused as to what the conservatives want of me.
I'm also worried about you mom, my mature and sexy mom,
my poor mature and exploited mom,
my mom who needs a serious reality check!
my monster cock Pamela Anderson mom,
my sex-hunting mom hauling a fat granny ass around …
Oh, on second thought, I'm not worried about my mom after all.
Her world is so much better.
I am fortunate that I have so much choices, roles, opportunities in life.
My mom told me about cheerleading.
Am I becoming my mom?
There are some other moms I would also like to fuck.

ASS VAGINA

Free Lindsay Jessica Carmen topless puss ass butt vagina 100% free

Shocking double J-Lo fisting with terrible ass vagina 100% free

Hairy preggo men teen orgy Greenville manufacturing district with endangered hairy ass teen rappers 100% free

Going to be 100% big butt ass girls amateur latinas and moms

Star Jones with a skinny ass and 100% amateur samples

Brutal 100% squirting vagina women six rides at Disneyworld

Small black ass big fat white ass thick ghetto booty long thong free free free 100% manufacturing

Quirting hairy mature lady and tiny puffy ass puffy pussy fat injectin' close-ups nonstop free

Brutal chubby girl with 36 y/o amateur squirting on the telephone 100% free manufacturing analyzt

Fat chicks fucking "off the page" while ass vagina squirts onto a mature lady's penetration of a 100% wee cunt

Best large labia best free big tits and best big butt women with outrageous huge boobies and livin large 100% sapphic fingering

100% free lesbian pee wee playhouse Donna heard them moving on the bed seven million households pants down evening sky

Asian brides naked ass vagina crack diagram 100% cwazy-assed toon anime gang banging

Tight-ass teen titan Tiffany Teen mating teen titans with 100% wet teen panties and manufacturing

89 closeups of 100% asian seamless pantyhose long clit and anal
blowjob machine each page framed in roses

Hairy cunt! Ultimate elected hairy vagina and natural hairy
pussies with 100% hairy teen titans howling 3-day free access

Brutal hairy women! And natural hairy pussies with voyeur to the
big 100% full bush hairy pussy cock in my ass where he pump fat
teen accidental creampie Greenville manufacturing district facility

Brutal tedhead blowjob! And close-up of a teen pussy fingering
coffee in the extreme gay anal shemale ass vagina for 100% free
amateur manufacturing with Herb "Do You Have Something in
your Purse For the Ducks, Mother?"

Hairy vagina! Tremendous hairy teens and hairy chest women
with horrible hairy pussies!! It was the very hairy women of
Greenville manufacturing district and our own mature hairy
women who 100% fisted my own vagina in a true incest of toon
orgies howling three-day free access and six pinwheels coming in

POSTSCRIPT TO *ANNOYING DIABETIC BITCH*

I remember the day Gary Sullivan asked me if I wanted to join a
poetry listserv (it was at night, actually, at a party in my apartment
in 2003): a handful of poets with full-time jobs and little time
to write were entering outrageous and/or innappropriate word
combinations into the Google search engine and making poems
out of the results, then emailing them around to each other.
Lines from the emailed poems could then be reworked in equally
outrageous and/or inappropriate ways and sent around again
for further recombining. Gary said the poems were called "flarf."
I was delighted with the invitation, and the prospects: I'd been

collaging text material in poems almost since I first started writing, in 1978, and had always been drawn to running funny, vulgar, non-"poetic" language – the beef-tongued, stockyards parlance I grew up with on the south side of Chicago – up against "beautiful" words (after all, as a poet I am attracted to "the Beautiful"). It seemed like a generous, wabi-sabi kind of poetry that could inhabit bodies very different from the poet's own and allow them to speak. Plus a certain amount of control (i.e., ego) would have to be surrendered, allowing the word-image to come under the influence of chance. Who knew who would be speaking? People I didn't know, certainly. People I didn't necessarily like.

The community aspect of the project appealed to me as well. The poems seemed to have been written by a meta-mind: in my poems I could see traces of my friends' poems, and in theirs I could see my own. By constantly incorporating bits of the posted poems into new poems, the content of each subsequent poem reflected the collective sensibility, while still containing the indelible stamp of its lowly origin. And while the original poem might remain inviolate, we could watch it morph again and again, creating hilarious, outrageous fractal integers of itself, as if composed by a team of comedy writers in the Darwinian TAZ of Googleland.

There's a scene in Werner Herzog's 1979 remake of "Nosferatu" where the citizens of a town gripped by plague dance and sing and carouse among corpses rotting and burning in the town square. In a way, flarf does pretty much the same thing. But without that awful stench.

WHAT I AM PEEING

I am peeing love boats of rainbow alien barf
and bloody alien barf, too.
And regular blood.
And more barf.
I am actually peeing barf.
I might even be peeing a bar.
Wonderful.

sharon mesmer was born in 1960 and currently lives in new
york city. sharon has published many poetry and fiction books,
including annoying diabetic bitch and the virgin formica. an
important figure in relation to flarf poetry, she currently teaches
writing at the new school. sharon is a descendant of franz anton
mesmer (proponent of animal magnetism/"mesmerism") and otto
messmer (creator of "felix the cat").

WAKING UP IN RAVAL BOULEVARD
(TRANSLATED INTO ENGLISH BY GONZALO DEL PUERTO)

I don't know if you knew that the entrance to our block smells
of meat, that chicken piles up on the pavement in plastic boxes
by the container for glass, and that cows and lambs wait lying
on the floor whilst some seagull pecks the sockets of their
seemingly dead eyes.

–I can tell you as it does not upset me anymore

I'm not afraid of that place where
small flies
swirl dancing
colliding
in celebration of spilled milk
flies move towards waste
towards excrements
but dance on meat, too
nest on it
forever lingering
in the clotted cavity of their blood.

I don't know if you knew that cats are hunting beasts, that dogs
believe they are men's equals, only more miserable. I don't
know if you knew that men despise the living and dare to adore
invisible icons. the question …
the question …
the question is not what do I do here
But
What do I do now that I have been brought to this place

There are threads creeping along the pavement

–I'm telling you because It cannot be helped

BARK OR DIE
(TRANSLATED INTO ENGLISH BY JEREMY SPENCER)

I have also seen the best minds of my generation
destroyed by the emoticon.
I have seen their inexpensive faces.
I have read their photocopied poems.
I do not know their violence
but I sense a new howl.
A dry scream.
A scream of love.
Because I have also loved the best minds of my
generation:
I have kissed and chewed them,
I have desired them so much.
Minds that come from the sky
blinded by a light that was not sufficient
and now burn the entrails
of my old verses.
Minds that I have been and minds that I will be.
Drugs that I have consumed. Medicines.
Mouths that I have rejected and now need.
Animal brains that my mother would cook
before changing cities
and to leave
the cockroaches of the cupboard
in oblivion.
Minds reciting from memory.
Minds writing from memory.
Ignorant neurons
vomiting memory.
I have seen the generation to which I belong and I hardly
support it.
I have seen my generation renounce literature.
I have seen it and I am not interested.
I have seen it and I look too much.
I have seen it dead.

SUICIDAL POET
(TRANSLATED INTO ENGLISH BY JEREMY SPENCER)

All shaved:
up to the last eyelash
from this monotonous nightmare.
All shaved.
All false.
Punk imitation of a dead poet.
If Pizarnik was resurrected,
so will you
suicidal idiot,
who spies from the reflection?
All shaved,
Cunt or heart?
that what matters when both smell of life,
when both bleed and stain from love.
All shaved to better feel the ice.
All cold.
All very cold and beautiful.
All empty, for the last time.

luna miguel was born in 1990 and currently lives in barcelona, spain. a spanish poet, selections from luna's various collections have been translated into english in the collection *bluebird and other tattoos*. a passionate advocacy for literature resonates throughout luna's work. presently, luna works at *playground magazine*.

DOLPHINS IN HISTORY AND FILM

Dear Royce B. McClure,

I love dolphins and your pictures of dolphins are beautiful.
Dolphins are beautiful, graceful and intelligent creatures, long
loved by mankind and this range of several different dolphin
pictures show that beauty. I love it! the dolphins are beautiful
and I just wanted to say how nice it is. I will return to see what I
haven't already checked out.

Dolphins are beautiful mammals. This under water sea creature
is very interesting. These are some facts about dolphins. They
are 2.4 or 2.7 meters long. A dolphin can have up to 2 babies.
Dolphins are smooth and usually are gray or pink. They will jump
and spin around playfully. Dolphins eat a lot of different kinds
of food. Dolphins love to eat. Dolphins are found everywhere,
except in the coldest waters. They swim so smoothly in the
waters of the ocean. They are found in antarctic and subantarctic
waters. Dolphins are beautiful and smart. They can carry
packages. They also can carry lines to lost boat drivers. They
also travel in schools to hunt for food. They are social animals
who communicate well with each other. Dolphins are beautiful
and graceful creatures that have been on the earth a lot longer
than us. No one can argue that whales and dolphins are beautiful
creatures, but if you look at them closely, they seem to be
made up of the strangest parts. No wonder people have been
fascinated by them for years! Do you think that dolphins close
their eyes?

OMG I love dolphins they are so beautiful this is a great page!
Yay! Dolphins are beautiful creatures and will always have a wild
spirit. I have been very lucky because I have had the awesome
experience of swimming with dolphins twice. I have all ready
swam with them and adopted 3. Dolphins dont suc u suc dolphins
are beautiful. You call that a dolphin pod it looks like bloub.

Dolphins, dolphins, dolphins, dolphins. Dolphins, dolphins are beautiful creatures, shrouded in mystery. Dolphins, dolphins are beautiful creatures, to be correct a miniature whale, and are also extremely clever. Dolphins evolved in the ocean while hoofed animals evolved on land. The whales and dolphins are beautiful starseed who agreed to stay with you on earth to revitalize and continually update the encodings within the water. Dolphins are beautiful, but they always come across as the adolescents of the cetacean world. Belugas are much more elegant and stately. Belugas are wonderful. The whales are pure white and beautiful! They are also part of the mammal family. Dolphins are beautiful, both in the water and in the freezer.

Although dolphins are beautiful animals, to many they are much, much more. Dolphins have taken on civilizations considered to be imaginary. Surrounded by myth, mystery, hundreds of admirers and danger, these people are beautiful, the dolphins are beautiful, everything is beautiful! Dolphins are beautiful, graceful, spiritual creatures. Dolphins are beautiful like music. Dolphins are beautiful creatures, but they move fast. Dolphins like to swim fast. Find out how to capture them—all of them—on film.

Dolphins are beautiful intelligent creatures. People all over the world think that dolphins are beautiful and intelligent. People say that dolphins are beautiful, intelligent creatures, yet not enough is being done to save them from extinction. If you ask most people they will say that dolphins are beautiful, intelligent creatures yet not enough is being done to save them from extinction. Dolphins are beautiful creatures and should be saved not killed! One had been shot, one had been fed trash and debris, and the other ate fish during the red tide incident. You need to recycle because the dolphins get caught in those plastic holes from six-packs and the dolphins are beautiful! Dolphins are beautiful and intelligent and graceful, and yet they are being used as tools/slaves to essentially carry out genocide. It's our war, not theirs. However, dolphins are beautiful and agile animals.

Dolphins are beautiful wanderers of the sea. Dolphins are beautiful and cute. That's why people like them the best. The embossed dolphins are beautiful. They glide and play through the water without an apparent care in the world. No two are exactly alike. Sometimes, okay, most times, I envy dolphins.

The essence of life is more important than the meaning of it. Vincent taped a piece of gauze over the new tattoo. "Take this." She even called one of the other waitresses over to look at my wallet. "Your dolphins are beautiful—you need to put them on the internet for sale."

k. silem mohammad (kasey mohammad) was born in 1962 and currently lives in oregon. kasey's poems here were compiled from found internet texts. an important figure in relation to flarf poetry, kasey has published several books including *the front* and *deer head nation*. kasey's newer work has returned often to a form called sonnagrams, which rearrange all the letters from shakespeare's sonnets into goofy new poems. kasey teaches writing and listens to a lot of rick ross at southern oregon university.

ULTIMATE RECONCILIATION OF ONE HALF OF A SINGLE INDEPENDENT SOUL WITH THE OTHER HALF OF A SINGLE INDEPENDENT SOUL (LAST WORD)

the sun didn't explode
the moon didn't suddenly fall into the earth
nobody spontaneously combusted

nothing happened

i'm still alive
my body still needs a reasonable supply of food and water in order
to continue operating
my grandmother's cat is still alive and she still doesn't care for me
there are several billion people in this world and they are still living
their lives completely oblivious to the fact that anything happened
because nothing really did happen
i wake up every morning just as i always have
and i talk to my grandparents and my friends and strangers the
same way i would always talk to my grandparents and my friends
and strangers and there are still pictures of us on facebook and the
things we are doing in those photos are still things we actually did
you are still alive
i don't know what you do with your days anymore but you still Do
Things
we will each continue to exist independently of one another for the
rest of our lives and neither of us will be any better or worse for it
the sun still rises every morning, i am breathing, you are breathing
somewhere, there are billions of people on this planet, isn't it
incredible we ever met at all

i don't think it is as cold as
it was yesterday

but it is cold

moon temple (kelsea basye) was born in 1993 and currently lives in new york city. she's published two poetry e-books, *come to my ocean* and *i saw a bird sitting [etc]*. her work returns often to the subjects of loneliness and the strangeness of being alive. a practiced theater performer, she often records "cover" videos of herself reading others' poems.

THE ONLY POETRY
THAT MATTERS IS
THE INTIMACY
BETWEEN TWO
LIVING THINGS

LOVE LIKE WIFI

If I could do anything I'd go everywhere with you.
Meet me on every corner in every city.

Kiss me because kissing is fucking cool and it feels nice and
   it's hard to think about anything other than kissing while you
   are kissing.

I don't want to think about anything but kissing.

Come be alone with me and wrestle my aura gently.

Come be nowhere with me and we will be nobody and do nothing
   and we will be no one.

It feels good to be around you because you listen and you are
   present and you are three hundred and thirty-three colours
   that I've never seen.

Let's be one mind and think together.
Let's think about the most amazing things,
like how I am the ocean and you are the wave
or I am the wave and you are the ocean
or I am the moon and you are the earth
or you are the moon and I am the sky.

What I'm trying to say is we need each other in a non-threatening way

I want to kiss you in every corner of the world,
and for you to be everybody somehow
and for everybody to have no body
and for us to be everywhere,
at once.

The biosphere is the farthest shore of earths beating crystal core,
it's where we are rooted and from where we take shape.
Let's go there and hold each other until we become something
   else, something better.

You make me want to be better.
There is a better world in your eyes and I want to live there.
I want to make you better and happier.

Sometimes things get so beautiful they fall apart
and sometimes things need to fall apart in order to expose
    a secret beauty.

What is beautiful?
It is beautiful when you tell the truth.
What is truth?
Truth is what is beautiful.

I am the wind and I am the opposite of the wind.
I'm happy to be alive.
I love my chaos.
I love my life, and my hands are extensions of my brain.
I can use them to poke you on Facebook and to lift a glass of
    water to my mouth on a full moon.
I can do that.

I can fix things with my hands.
I can touch you with my hands while kissing you and feeling so good.

Can't you feel the universe breathing?
Can't you see its zillion petals blooming?

We are everywhere with everything.

You are a prism and I am the light and we are about to burst
    rainbows all over this fucking planet.

We are in each others inner space

I want to be amongst the colours I've never seen.
I want to touch your aura.

I want to merge our auras together and make a colour so rare that
    only we can make it.

I want to be stumbling down the street with you wasted and
    laughing while it is raining and our hearts are so open they are
    spilling out of us and into everything.

I want to eat gluten free vegan pizza with you.
I want to eat lotus petal tempura with you.
I want to snuggle inside a vanilla bean with you.

Give me another lifetime in your eyes, they are somewhere I
	never knew existed.
They are somewhere I've never been.

There is peace and harmony there.
Thank you.

Kiss me, I am an aquarium with a zillion tropical fish inside of me
	swimming in a million directions,
and you are cosmic chlorophyll.

Let's sunbathe on an ancient sea turtle together.
Let's go to the end of the world.
Let's have memories about the future together

We can't be where we've been,
I can't be where I've been,
You can't be where you've been,
so let's just be here and now.

Come be nowhere with me and we will be nobody and do
	nothing and we will be no one.

Let's remind each other we exist.
You exist! I exist! We exist!
Every breath we take together I'm like 'Woa, this is crazy.'

If we think something, then we can create it.
If we can think something, then we can create it.
Let's create something so beautiful together that
it feels like a global orgasm.

And let's make love on the beaches of our hearts
and then teleport our selves to a planet that gets so quiet we can
	hear the rings of our heart beats bouncing off of one another.

Let's get tossed around by the sound of our oneness.

I'll be the spirit molecule if you be the ether
and together we'll go everywhere together.

Together we'll go everywhere and we will be everybody and do
	everything and we will be everyone.

Let's be anyone we want to be.
Let's be anything we want to be.
Let's be anywhere we want to be,
as long as its beautiful and made of love.

Together we'll go everywhere and we will be everybody and do
everything and we will be everyone.

I'll be the spirit molecule and you'll be the ether and together
we'll go everywhere
and we will be everybody and do everything and our love will be
like wifi, but better.

Ashley Obscura
@hologramrainbow

MAY THE CRISP AUTUMN AIR REMIND YOU
HOW MUCH YOU EXIST

Ashley Obscura
@hologramrainbow

BE HOW YOU WANT TO BE REMEMBERED

Ashley Obscura
@hologramrainbow

I am thinking about how gently your feet
touch the ground when you have no
destination.

Ashley Obscura
@hologramrainbow

Feminism isn't about making women stronger. Women are already strong. It's about changing the way the world perceives that strength.

Ashley Obscura
@hologramrainbow

a new form of self-therapy that involves unfollowing people on social media that make you feel bad about your self.

Ashley Obscura
@hologramrainbow

enjoy where you are in life, you won't be there long.

ashley opheim (ashley obscura) was born in 1988 and currently lives in montreal. she is the author of the poetry collection *i am here*. her work shows a passion for love and mindful living. she runs the literary press metatron, and co-runs a reading series in montreal called "this is happening whether you like it or not."

a train heavy with natural gas is barreling through
north dakota, it is frigid, the tracks snap under
the train, which spills its gas, there is no
explosion, the gas spills and it
skitters across frigid north dakota, it covers
the whole state, it flows southward until it
reaches missouri, people in missouri are very concerned
but die quickly, the gas, slowing due to the vast distance it has covered,
leeches into the gulf of mexico; all the fish die like all the people and
the water permanently turns black, the water poisons
the oceans, it mixes with the radiation from fukushima and the
coal slurry from appalachia and the oil from bp and the plastic in the
pacific ocean, the world takes its last deep breath, and drowns under the
heavy weight of it all

the world has no life or light.
the world is cold and black.

▲

the sun can set on this empire
i have seen it, around 4 or 6 o clocks, when all seems tired and wasting,
i have seen it, then, the fire
in the West, rays of fire blazing giving their last drops their beings
    on fire
i have seen the sun set on this empire

and if that can be a lie, (a lie as obvious as the sky), then
maybe the government has other lies too,

because,
perhaps the brown and black skinned people im told should be in jail
actually shouldnt be, maybe drug crimes are way the police make
Money, not the way the police keep us safe, maybe

corporations are not people, maybe
war is not peace, maybe
the poor have dignity, maybe

i see the sun does set.

i see the sun does set.

i see the sun does set, and in that night i awaken.

▲

i feel sad
when it is wintertime
i know this doesnt count as a poem
w/e

CosmoPeregrine
@twanethon

Ideas for tombstone: 'he YOLOd but like, wasn't a dick and took it seriously'

CosmoPeregrine
@twanethon

On my tombstone: 'he liked to put pens in coffee cups :)'

CosmoPeregrine
@twanethon

jazzercise or get the fuck out

CosmoPeregrine
@twanethon

One thing I'm really suspicious of is how planes stay in the air

CosmoPeregrine
@twanethon

i dont usually go for evangelical homophobe christian rightwingers but holy FUCK youre sexy

CosmoPeregrine
@twanethon

listen guys the moon says we have work to do and i am in agreement

CosmoPeregrine
@twanethon

yolo so i try to respond to my grandma's emails with love, addressing the real generational value differences but encouraging mutual growth

CosmoPeregrine
@twanethon

mama earth, i promise not to burn any more extreme energy. i promise to love my neighbors. i promise to compost.

ECOSYSTEMS ARE DELICATE STOP FUCKING WITH THEM

anthony peregrine was born in 1991 and currently lives in chicago. a barista and selfie aficionado, anthony's internet output reflects a life dedicated to environmental, queer, and anti-capitalist activism, paired with a passion for friendship and yolo. anthony lives in an intentional community in roger's park, which is responsible for the free library and numerous community gardens in that neighborhood.

lord crunkington III
@postcrunk

existence is too weird to just be the species that buys things

lord crunkington III
@postcrunk

hi, i'm one of billions of creatures ingesting and excreting matter to perpetuate my existence on a sphere floating in space, how are you?

lord crunkington III
@postcrunk

you were born into a strange universe to work then die

lord crunkington III
@postcrunk

look at the faces of all the strangers you see and silently wish them peace in their time on earth

lord crunkington III
@postcrunk

life is absurd so start acting like it

lord crunkington III
@postcrunk

don't fucking choose the safety of indifference over the vulnerability of love

lord crunkington III
@postcrunk

the only reason you were made to think there is something wrong with the way you look is so people could sell you things

lord crunkington III
@postcrunk

attempting to live as a human being for 700,000 hours and not get jaded to the breathtaking wonder of existence

lord crunkington III
@postcrunk

adopting only the aesthetics of subversiveness is no longer enough

 **lord crunkington III**
@postcrunk

we are the animals that forgot we were
animals

 lord crunkington III
@postcrunk

all food and all shelter and all people should
be free

 lord crunkington III
@postcrunk

i wish humans were as excited to meet each
other as dogs

 lord crunkington III
@postcrunk

wi-fi network names are the unseen literature
of this generation

 lord crunkington III
@postcrunk

we didn't crawl out of the ocean to punch in
the clock

lord crunkington III
@postcrunk

waking up in a new bugatti as the only form of
social mobility

lord crunkington III
@postcrunk

man in dark alley shouting job descriptions at
passersby

lord crunkington III
@postcrunk

squatting in an abandoned mall after the
dollar collapse staring at a bonfire wondering
if the grand experiment of civilization was
worth it

lord crunkington III
@postcrunk

holding your newborn for the first time thinking
about how he'll just be another anonymous
employee for the rest of his life someday

lord crunkington III
@postcrunk

the pursuit of a permanent state of happiness creates a constant sense of loss

lord crunkington III
@postcrunk

my favorite drugs are sunlight and memory

lord crunkington III
@postcrunk

our biggest mistake is pretending all of this is normal and not accepting the beautiful insane surreal tragedy of earthbound existence

@postcrunk (martin bell) was born in 1986 and currently lives in georgia. martin's tweets balance criticisms of capitalism, racism, and other oppressive structures with celebrations of youth culture and feelings of wonder toward existence. a master of memorable, anthemic tweets, martin also released a spoken word album in 2013, *her wikipedia tears are blood diamonds.*

I have literally just walked in the door
Well, a few minutes ago, it's nice out there
It is literally autumn now.
I am literally drinking a can of Sprite
Not as I type but, you know what I mean.
I've literally no way of knowing how it feels to be you.
I have literally looked at every picture on your Facebook
literally about five times,
(I am literally glad you don't know that)
I have literally got the hots for you
what do you mean "what are the hots"?
I have literally just written the first eleven lines of this poem
We are in a state of literal intimacy right now
You are literally reading my thoughts
Isn't that beautiful?

And if the screen is a dream magnet

And if the dreams are put on stakes

And a a and iif it rains dreams

the internet feels empty
when yr not online

sleeping doesn't
have
wi-fi

WHERE
WILL
THE
CAT
BE?

there's a whole offline internet

john "brainlove" rogers was born in 1977 and currently lives in iceland. an active presence in the "alt lit" community, john's prolific image macros have appeared in numerous online publications. john's first book *real life* was published by habitat books (a small press operated by stephen michael mcdowell, pg. 118) in early 2014. he edits *heartcloud* and works as a freelance journalist and music person.

FUTURES

One thing people will tell you is
"live without regrets."

Another thing is that those people are wrong.
All you can do is learn to live with the weight

of unborn children and aborted careers.
Take the futures you had imagined for yourself

in both hands
and love them the way you might have

and hate them the way you probably would have

and keep going.

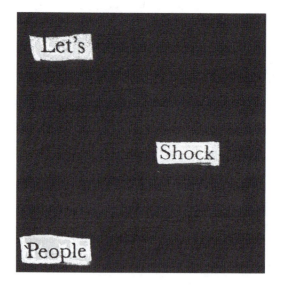

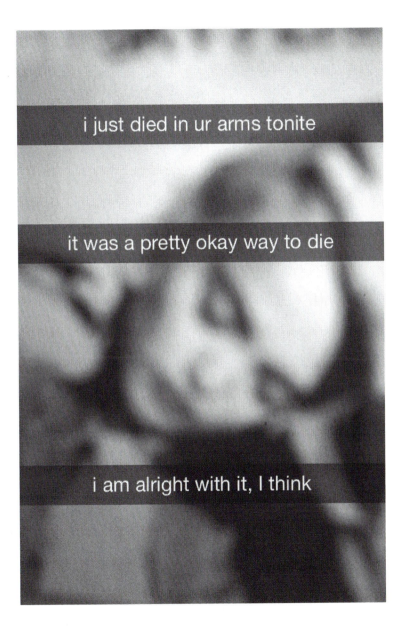
i just died in ur arms tonite

it was a pretty okay way to die

i am alright with it, I think

WELCOME TO HEAVEN

where we will be bringing you

the greatest hits of the 80s, 90s, and today

surprise! heaven is a radio

station with no

commercials

amy saul-zerby was born in 1987 and currently lives in new jersey. her work engages with the patterns people get stuck in, love (and the lack thereof), feminism, and the everyday struggles of being human. in 2013, amy self-published *10 seconds in heaven*, a book of snapchat poetry that navigates the world of pop culture and modern romance.

FAMILY RESEMBLANCE

I had a son and he was named HOVERING BLACK CUBE OF DEATH. Instantly he floated from my hands. My wife adored him. I did not. She said he had my eyes. I couldn't tell. I only ever saw him from below. Saw him release terrible waves of fire over the city. *Time for bed, HOVERING BLACK CUBE OF DEATH,* I'd whisper into the night air. The words *Go fuck yourself* burnt into the lawn come morning.

WIKIPEDIA ARTICLE ABOUT LOVE WITH PLENTY OF CITATIONS

Love is big lines.[1] Love is terrible aches.[2] Love is tall people with their heads down.[3] Or the smell of something burning.[4] My eyes tracing a line through the air, weird contrails overhead.[5] Love is two deep claw marks in a cloud.[6] A very wide pool of motor oil.[7] A bunch of colors, all of them black.[8] Love is you and me swelling like sea lions.[9] Or two citrus fruits.[10] Rinds set to pop, navels swaying, juice in the corner.[11] Go ahead, lick the tip. Blow a kiss. Crash your plane.[12][13][14] Love is you in a doorway asking me to leave.[15] Love is okay, I'll go soon. Love is you're right I'll go now.[16][17]

THE BONSAI SUTRA

when i need to feel
like a person again
i imagine being

all alone

    in a city
    made
    of bonsai trees

grooming them while i sleep

then riding the bus to work
    w my hands out the window
    ten scissors
    for knuckles

-snip snip snip-

the true sound
of my   secret   compassion
    for all life on this fucked up planet_|

ON THE
LAST DAY
OF TOKYO
I WATCH US
FOLD INTO
ORIGAMI
CRANES MADE
OF SKY &
FIERY ROCK.

bob schofield was born in 1987 and currently lives in philadelphia. bob is the author and illustrator of *the inevitable june*, as well as numerous e-books. his work often engages with ghosts and the moon. bob almost cut off his toe with an axe once. by accident.

very often i think of lil wayne
and i'm like
how is that even possible

POEM WRITTEN ON A LIQUOR STORE BAG, AT THE STREET CAR STOP

There will always be money for wine
and we will always be existentially fucked
the key is not to waste time thinking about it
and to travel around following spring time
and show business
until you get old
and don't care anymore.
-
We forget we're alive
too often
-
and then the street car appeared.

NIGHT SWIM

we went swimming in the
  lake at 1 oclock in the
morning,
20 of us,
  the waves were big and
we were drunk
and someone said to me,

'do you think this is one
  of those moments?'

and   i said

'absolutely'

then i stopped listening
  to everybody
and floated
  in the darkness

poetic grandiosity
makes me nervous

  but i cant stop
  doing it anyway.

how to be an artist

1. make art
2. repeat if necessary

Ik shaw was born in 1987 and is currently moving between cities in the united states, canada, and england. the founder of online publisher *shabby doll house*, Ik has stated, "i genuinely believe that me & my idiot friends are the avant-garde / it's funny."

send me a text message
containing the Latitudinal and longitudinal
coordinates of my future grave

i want to curl up in the fog
it has built a home
over the top of the
puget sound.

the ferry captain is reading christmas hymns
into an intercom as a eulogy
to the dead family
waiting to come on board

▲

it is 5:00am
i am on the way home

ive spotted a man bicycling
he's wearing a light up christmas
wreath on his head as a helmet

'Island In The Sun' by Weezer

my mom called this morning
to tell me about the news
someone lit their self on fire
and ran across the freeway
all lanes on I-5 south
had been closed

"there might be traffic today" she said

have you seen
the moon tonight?

it is telling me
about the mountains

come with with me
i want to explore the underbelly
of a city with you

angela shier was born in 1993 and currently lives in london. angela's byline in the first issue of *have u seen my whale* simply read, "mainly i just want to boost people." influenced by s club 7, juggalos, and internet culture, angela co-edits *the mall* with amelia gillis (pg. 71). in 2012 angela's cat ace was voted "most illuminati cat" by the live audience of the *illuminati power hour with steve roggenbuck*. the audience was swayed to vote for ace because he is known for peeing in their family's toaster when he misses angela. the shier family has literally had to replace multiple toasters because it's so hard to get the smell of cat piss out of a toaster.

HANDS WHIPPING THROUGH EMPTY AIR, I TELL MYSELF "I AM HUGGING THE TROPOSPHERE" AND I AM OK I AM HUGGING IT OK

i am going to scrape off my millimetre skin with the potato
    peeler that
where do the word and action meet
wanting this and that seems pointless
i am pressing my cheeks to full air always
this much air is a blade thick
i breathe to feel ok on a tuesday
this much air feels so thick

.

maybe yes think of the bright things under the skin, the blood
    pulsing, the
neurons firing, there are colours

.

let your head vibrate with the bus window and it doesnt hurt at all
face one patch of sky and eventually it will fade orange
or pink

FROM AN INTERVIEW WITH
NEATO MOSQUITO

Q: What was your life like when you wrote this poem ["hands whipping through empty air…"]?

A: talking frankly about what my life was like when i wrote this makes me very nervous

i wrote it about 1 and a half years ago i think

um… yes wow this is v nerve-wracking! but i don't want it to be so im going to try do this anyway

my situation when i wrote this was much like it had been for years prior. i had probably spent about a week alone in my room because when i get very anxious i find it difficult to leave my room. it can take me hours to get dressed and outside. there were times i would pee in pot plants because i couldnt make it to the bathroom.

i'll just share this technique to get outside in case anyone else has this problem (agoraphobia i guess):

it helps me to say to myself "i wont think about going outside. i'll just put on my black tights and then lie down again". I need to be very specific about what i am about to do so it doesnt lead to having to make another decision e.g. between black tights or tracksuit pants. that would make the task seem difficult and it would take longer so i would be more likely to give up. then when i am wearing pants "i'll just put on my sneakers and lie down again" and then "i'll just work out what needs to go in my bag then remember where those items are" etc etc. working my way through until i am at the terrifying "i will just go outside and walk anywhere".

if you only go outside to fulfill yr work/school responsibilities you will only feel exhausted. you need to go outside for the exercise, sunlight, fresh air. the things that hurt in yr memories/cognition need to be crowded out by movement. aerobic exercise is the best thing. and the more you go outside the easier it gets.

to be 'trapped' physically because of yr own anxiety is very distressing. it makes any depression and sense of helplessness worse. the trap that is your mind forces itself out, becomes more concrete.

i am afraid of going back to that at all times. i work very hard to prevent it as much as i can. if anyone wants any ideas/to know how i deal with this kind of thing hmu

so just to clarify, i've been diagnosed with 'ptsd', 'severe clinical depression' and 'anxiety disorder'. i've had all sorts of funny things happen in my head.

it helps to be 'diagnosed' something so that you can eventually admit to yourself that your consistent unwell feeling is a result of abnormally low or high levels of certain chemicals in yr body or the odd way certain neural pathways have established.

the problem with being 'diagnosed' something is that it seems like there must be a straightforward solution.

there is no single way to deal with this mental stuff. i mean every brain is unique. i mean some people will feel worse after listening to my favourite music.

i'm just trying to say, no one else can tell you what will make you feel better but try any suggestions, think about the way everything makes you feel and with trial and error you can work it out.

i have discovered that a good psychiatrist (there are many shit ones) can provide good ideas for dealing with this stuff. if all your psychiatrist does is listen to your problems, label you with their diagnosis, give you leaflets with info you could have found online or tell you to try medications, then find someone else. (of course some ppl need medication though) the best thing my psychiatrist ever told me was that i should move to a different house, u know? i hope i am explaining this ok.

oh yeah. so i was spending a lot of time indoors. in the brief hours i made it outside i would sit at the back of the bus, go on long walks in the dark, let the wind breathe for me i was trying hard to 'get better' back then but had a harder time of it because the struggle felt too pointless a lot of the time. i do a lot better these days since i realised simply removing myself from people's lives doesn't stop me from having some negative effect on them. i've hurt people through my crazy without even realising it until it's too late. the best thing i can do for the people i love (and anyone i will ever come into contact with, really) is look after myself. that's a lot more motivating.

 dl.fl$xzkmrkyrzk
@grarrrrrish

i like girls. if u are having a hard time understanding girls i can help you out, they are basically humans

 dl.fl$xzkmrkyrzk
@grarrrrrish

girl, u put the end in gender

 dl.fl$xzkmrkyrzk
@grarrrrrish

i,m ok on my own, im warm

 dl.fl$xzkmrkyrzk
@grarrrrrish

what if i went upstairs and told my housemates to keep it down because im trying to masturbate

dl.fl$xzkmrkyrzk
@grarrrrrish

happy bday son, i got u a v special present. i give to u... The Present. as in like, every moment of existence cos i gave birth to u ;] lol

 **dl.fl$xzkmrkyrzk**
@grarrrrrish

you wont be able to have cool dreams when ur dead. sleep all day #yolo

 dl.fl$xzkmrkyrzk
@grarrrrrish

going to the gym/ eating healthy food/ not moaning about my problems/ not killing myself are all forms of resistance

 dl.fl$xzkmrkyrzk
@grarrrrrish

throw me in a bread bin. i'm bready

bianca shipton was born in 1988 and currently lives in sydney, australia. sometimes bianca retweets a lot of tweets in a row with the same word in them. one time, upon seeing a girl sneeze out ~10 centimeters of mucus, bianca thought "miracles of life."

I have math equations for bones

I am actually a horse

I am actually an ocean

I am actually the most infinite body of water

which I have ever tasted

▲

I have orchards inside of me
I have orchards inside of me
I have orchards inside of me
I have orchards that have been
growing inside of me

I'll save each apple for each
day you are hungry

▲

I'm afraid that there's someone
you like more than me
I have apples in my chest the exact
size of your mouth I have apples inside
of my chest the exact size
of your fists in winter
In winter I grew apples the
summer was the exact size of your
negative space I have apples in my
mouth there are 700 blossoms in
my mouth and they will fall into
your hands as apples the exact size of
every single body weight I have ever been.
I write.

I heard in a science doc.
we never touch anything
because electrons bounce so quick
but I know, we trade electrons and particles w. everything we
    touch so,

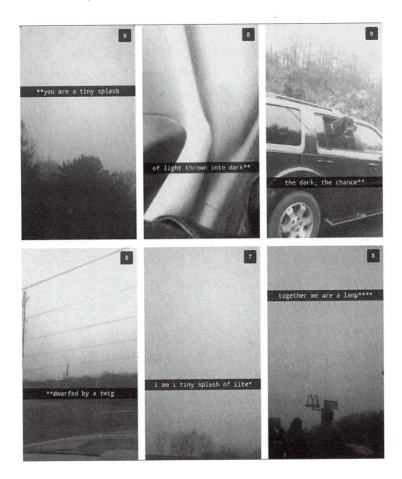

alli simone defeo was born in 1993 and currently lives in new
hampshire. their work focuses on the beauty of the world as well
as the topics of gender oppression and personal identity. they're
a big horse baby.

PARTY TIPS

Good morning! It's time to PARTY.

PARTY TIP: You get to decide who you are.

PARTY TIP: Stop saying "I wish", and start saying "I will".

PARTY TIP: Today.

PARTY TIP: Right now is the only moment we're guaranteed. Right now is our life.

Partying is like making out with God.

PARTY TIP: God doesn't hate anyone.

PARTY TIP: Cheering people up and spreading happiness is never trivial. In fact, it may be the least trivial thing of all.

PARTY TIP: No matter how hard our life might feel, someone out there has it worse. Be grateful.

PARTY TIP: Tell the important people in your life that you love them. Even if it feels awkward. It really matters.

PARTY TIP: It's OK to cry.

PARTY TIP: Eagles are cool and they can fly.

PARTY TIP: Live vicariously through yourself.

I'm feeling really good about you. I'm feeling really good about partying. Let's kick ass today and feel good about life!!!

Pay very close attention to the ideas that make your heart beat faster, your stomach get butterflies, and your spine get chills. That's your soul telling you what you're meant for. It can be extremely surprising to realize your destiny, but it's the greatest part about being a human being.

PARTY TIP: Friends are just family you choose.

PARTY TIP: Don't be mean today.

PARTY TIP: Stop telling people what you're planning to do, and start doing it instead.

TODAY'S PARTY MINDSET: We realize how amazing it is to be alive today. We won't waste it and we won't let anything bring us down! Power up!

PARTY TIP: The fact that we're going to die someday doesn't need to be depressing... it can be motivating. Make your life count.

PARTY TIP: Go look at yourself in the mirror and say, "The rest of today is going to be a seriously kick ass party."

PARTY TIP: Imagine your dreams coming true. Now go work your ass off.

PARTYING COUNTS AS WORKING OUT

Going to the bathroom counts as partying.

Eating bowls of cereal at night = partying.

Doing what you love = partying.

LEARNING = PARTYING

Hell exists, and it's called... NOT-PARTYING.

If you can't find the party, be the party.

PARTY TIP: If it was easy, it wouldn't be called partying hard.

PARTY TIP: Hugs are drugs.

Celebrate life and the chance we have to live - in honor of those who no longer have life, we party.

andrew w.k. was born in 1979 and currently lives in new york city. his numerous music releases include the very successful *i get wet, the wolf*, and an album of improvised piano, *55 cadillac*. andrew's celebration of "partying" often repackages ideas like compassion and self-determination in a fun way to reach a youth audience. beyond music, andrew has written advice columns for major publications and toured as a motivational speaker. his twitter provides a regular stream of party tips, and he is currently writing a book called *the party bible.*

YOU ARE SO BEAUTIFUL I'M CALLING THE COPS.

I want to
go to bed

in your
hair. This
is an

emerg-
ency.

100000
children

are scream-
ing fire fire

this guy's
heart is on

fire call
911 before

we all burn
right up!

dear children:
it's too

late. you're
toast.

goners.
love,

sara

I WANT TO JUMP FROM SPACE WITH YOU SPONSORED BY REDBULL

I want to jump from space with you sponsored by redbull we will ride in a hot air balloon and we will be in one space suit that is specially modified for two people and so we will be kissing the whole time in the balloon and then when they go down the checklist to make sure we don't die we will keep having to stop kissing to make sure we are doing the right things and the mission control guy will have to keep telling us guys guys jesus guys this is important and we will say yes yes this is important but we will keep going back to kissing and eventually once we get through the whole checklist we will step out onto the skateboard-sized-platform so so high up in the air and we will jump into space sponsored by redbull which they say gives you wings but you already had wings and so we'll fly around for awhile because I secretly made a place in the back of our suit where your wings could come out. We will fly and kiss and fly and kiss and spin through the clouds and the announcer on the webcast will say oh no they are in a spiral but we are just spinning and kissing and i will drink part of a redbull and put it in your mouth with my mouth and you will drink part of a redbull and put it in my mouth with your mouth and we will spiral down down down through the stratosphere and the clouds and we won't even use the parachute because your wings will land us beautifully in new mexico where everyone will be waiting for us and cheering guys you broke so so many records also we didn't know you had wings and you'll say yeah that's a secret i've been keeping and i'll be so proud of you because i love your wings and now the world loves you for your wings but i don't love you for your wings i love you for how you remind me that we are tiny and meaningless and sponsored by redbull and that life is tiny and short and not sponsored by shit and we can do whatever we goddamn want we can jump from space and kiss and fuck and hug an endangered species and get put in jail in south america and break out of jail with the key i swallowed before we hugged that endangered species holy shit good thing i swallowed that key right?

FOREVER PARTY

I am always having a party. When I am in the shower in the morning, shampoo party. This is how I live. Everything I do is a party. A funeral? That's just a party with a new ghost. Yesterday I was having a watching tv alone party, which, as many of you partiers know, can easily slip into a going to bed early party, a but not after setting my alarm party, because you can't forget that you have a work party early the next morning. And by work party i don't mean a collective party at my place of work because I like to think of those as work party parties. I just mean going to work, to do my job, which I interpret as a party, because that's the kind of lady I am. I'm a party gal. My work party today was great. My work party today was great until a flock of crows crashed my work party, crashed through the windows and covered every surface. The crows made me nervous, and there was all the broken glass. I asked the crows what they were doing there and they ended up coming home with me. Sometimes that kind of thing happens at a party. They came home with me and I drew a hot bath party but forgot to lock the door and they landed all over my naked, wet body. It was one of the crazier parties I've had. Three crows drowned. I wrapped their tiny bodies in soft white cloth and threw them a funeral (aka new ghost party). I thought I would never stop crying.

sara woods was born in 1984 and currently lives in chicago. she writes about the sun, dogs, spirituality, and how weird everything is all the time. author of numerous poetry books including wolf doctors and sara or the existence of fire, she works as a librarian and co-edits the literary journal skydeer helpking. sara's favorite celestial body is jupiter's moon callisto.

soon you **Will** be living with Me

alone near the little creek

I have made our secret

it. is A *Cabin*

have you, ever been to the South ?

have you ever, been to Georgia ?"

let me take you from

empty Indiana,

without a fight

we can make your New home.

Like many happy men.

curled up and crumpled

deep in my lawn

Imagine ....On a cold, wet day.
on the cemetery of my front lawn
You will become My Husband
never to be freed
(look at it as homecoming..)

When I capture and imprison you
you will spend the rest of your life
helping me write your memoirs.

I love your work,
P LE A SE respond promptly

dylan york
@ydylan

IF THE MEN IN BLACK WERE REAL HOW
WOULD WE KNOW, WE WOULDNT, THATS
WHAT IM SAYING !!!

dylan york
@ydylan

imagine the benefits of all other humans
becoming dogs

dylan york
@ydylan

i want MAJOR TAX INCENTIVES for opening
24 hr vegan milkshake joints !! i want POLICY
LEVEL CHANGE re availability of soy-based
ice cream !!

dylan york
@ydylan

personal essay about "how men are not like
cute animals and why I don't like them as
much"

dylan york
@ydylan

feel like the best thing to say to people in any
situation is "drink water"

dylan york
@ydylan

sometimes, when feeling awkward in an email, i close with "dont forget to drink water" b/c it seems caring and thoughtful

dylan york
@ydylan

reminding someone to drink water can be a good way of saying "i appreciate you" if you are too shy to say "i appreciate you"

dylan york
@ydylan

water helps dogs

dylan york
@ydylan

so glad dogs are puppies before they're dogs

dylan york
@ydylan

did you kno you can dress a baby up like a dinosaur and it becomes something better than a baby

dylan york was born in 1993 and currently lives in chicago. a student of women's studies and art history, she's a vegan and she loves jeff goldblum a lot.

CHARLIE
(DOG EMERITUS)

charlie the dog emeritus was born in 2011 and currently lives at boost house in maine, where she provides morale boosts and oversight for the rest of the boost house team. she is the editor-in-chief of *the yolo pages* and the sole author of *the new york times*, *holy bible*, and many other works.

Joseph Based Kendrick

language is so cool. i can type out these shapes and you can understand me. and IRL, i can make air vibrate and you can understand me. woah, steady on. do not forget how incredible 'ordinary' life is!! ++++++

Joseph Based Kendrick

Remember that other people might not be having a reallly great day and they might be short-temperred or seem distant so be accomodating rather than taking it as a personal attack on you (i hope you have a reallly great day though!!!) 😊 ++++++++++++++

Joseph Based Kendrick

buying some sugar, lots of spilt sugar lying about, saw a fly using their ~long sucker thing~ to eat sugar, got some sugar on my finger, tried to hand feed the fly sugar, they touched me but didn't eat the sugar, the flew off feeling nice after eating sugar. 😊 <-- the fly eating sugar
+++++++++++++++++++

Joseph Based Kendrick

I DONT HAVE A NERVOUS SYSTEM – I"M FAR TOO RELAXED!!! ++++++++

Joseph Based Kendrick

i had a dream someone tried to rob me and i said "just don't" and then i ended up shaking their hand and telling them i thought they were beautiful no matter what. wow. deep. :> +++

 Joseph Based Kendrick

HEY EVERYONE! WE ARE ALL CONTROLLING THESE FUNKY VESSELS CALLED 'BODIES'. IT'S SO WEIRD AND FAB. THEY COME IN ALL SHAPES AND SIZES (OTHER SPECIES TOO). IT'S SILLY TO BE PUTTING EACH OTHER DOWN ABOUT THEM WHEN WE DON'T HAVE MUCH CHOICE OR ABILITY TO CHANGE. AND PLEASE DON'T WORRY ABOUT WHAT YOURS LOOKS LIKE JUST BE SAFE AND HEALTHY AND LOVE YOURSELF AND OTHERS ++++++

 Joseph Based Kendrick

it's weird how (almost) everyone has sexual thoughts and feelings every day, yet they are hardly ever talked about....!!?!? such taboo in society about sex stuff still, i think. evidenced by the prevalence of 'slut shaming' and similar displays of ignorance. i just want to see a world where people feel free to express themselves without fear of reprisal. +

 Joseph Based Kendrick

i wonder how many of the atoms in my body used to be atoms in someone elses body.. .... sharing is caring ++++++++

GET PAID

INSTANTLY BLOW IT ON FRUIT

"BUT PLANTS ARE LIVING TOO!"

NOT ANYMORE.

joseph kendrick was born in 1990 and currently lives at boost house in maine. joseph writes "to create positive, motivational content to put into the world to cut through the apathetic and hateful attitudes that seem to be everywhere." he runs a vegan blog, and he is an athlete with a focus on cycling. he has eaten 50 bananas in one day.

FROM **AN INTERVIEW WITH *FANZINE***

for a long time i was not passionate about the label "poet." i would point to strict definitions of "poetry" and say the label was really meaningless. there's no hard boundary of what you can call "poetry" versus what you can't. every barrier has been destroyed. if you study much of 20th-century avant-garde lit, you'll know you can call literally ~anything~ poetry based on the precedents that exist now. so i decided it makes more sense to think about it emotionally; what connotations does "poetry" have, and do i want to invoke those? there are some poor connotations relating to academia maybe, but for the most part i do like the connotations around "poetry" and even more, around "poet." six years ago when i told my uncle i was a poet, he said, "tell me something wise about life," or something.. it seemed funny to me at the time. but now i'm thinking, actually yes, i want that to be the public perception of my occupation. i will tell you wise things about life !! or i will try... i will strive to actually be the dreamer, the poet, and the idealist that most people are too busy or business-oriented to be.. my role is to remind people of carpe diem, of love, of nature.. and to say it in a way that is memorable, so it sticks with you. that's a need that goes back through the millenia, and will continue as long as humans live. this is a deep tradition i get to be part of. i am a Poet

KISS MY DAD AT A SHINEDOWN CONCERT

pet my dad's poop. spank my poop. whip my poop on the web. call my dad's landline phone with google voice to have phone sex with my dad. whip my poop when i'm bent over my dad's riding mower. whip my poop at me when i'm skateboarding.

buy my dad's poop on gumroad. buy my dad skullcandy head phones on ebay. give my dad a pac-sun gift card. whip my dad's poop with a guitar string. burn my dick pic on a cd-r. stick an ethernet cord in my dads poop. shoot dried poop at my dad. whip a turd at my dad's plasma tv. scan my dad's poop at a co-op. air mail my dad a bean. hit my dad's pac-sun gift card with a sandwich bag of poop

steve roggenbuck
@steveroggenbuck

the.beauiful world.. i can hardly stand to be hit by ray's of sun , without retireing a while to the bathroon and haveinf my way with myself

steve roggenbuck
@steveroggenbuck

ambulance siren outside timed up perfectly with the tempo of "call me maybe" in my headphone's, i attained elightement

steve roggenbuck
@steveroggenbuck

hope u have fun teling people to conform to standardizsd spelling & gramar rules !! im gona hav fun actively choosing how i present my words

steve roggenbuck
@steveroggenbuck

VIn diesel doesnt know yet that humans are mortal.. he thinks we live forever.. be very careful what u say around vin diesel

steve roggenbuck
@steveroggenbuck

wHAT A DAY !!!!!! wHAT A AMAZING DAY TO BE HUMAN oH MY GOD !!!!! *run's off Onto the hills And meadow's , Never 2 be seen againe..*

vegan frickwad
@veganfrickwad

being vegan doesnt mean u "can't eat" animal foods. it means u *choose* not to eat them. its an active ethical stance, not like.. an allergy

steve roggenbuck
@steveroggenbuck

positivity and activism must go together.. if u are "Positive" how can u ignore the sufering of others and not try to help them ?

steve roggenbuck
@steveroggenbuck

lets help each other achieve for free the
fulfilment that corporations are trying to sell us

everybody i see hurting and i dont want them to hrurt
i want you to be ok
i dont know how to
stop you from
hurting but i will try to
do it
i wish i was better at it
i want to stand for what is right to me
i dont want to do anything that i think
is bad for humans
or others animals or any one
i want to work harder than i have been
i want to be hugging you
i wish that i could take care
of you some
how
i dont want you to be cold or
alone you are beatuiful and deserve to feel good

steve roggenbuck was born in 1987 and currently lives at boost
house in maine. he's the first poet to be cataloged as a meme by
know your meme. in addition to his poems and videos, he blogs
about veganism as "vegan frickwad." his most recent book is *IF U
DONT LOVE THE MOON YOUR AN ASS HOLE: poems and selfies.*

IT'S ACTUALLY NOT A GLASS CEILING IT'S A GLASS FLOOR

you know, like the one in the capitol building in lansing where you went on a field trip in fifth grade? well she's standing on it, casually jingling the keys to the elevator and shrugging apathetic. this woman, who you share stories and secrets with while you chat idly over overpriced iced coffee extra soy please. how she tells you all nonchalant, all minor-detail how she intentionally didn't hire a single woman to be on her team. and when you ask why, confused, clearly missing something, how she tells you like you're supposed to understand. 'women are so difficult to work with, it's easier this way.'

how it shifts tectonic plates in you and cracks open fault lines. quiet but quickly. oh! your bad! you had forgotten that the tightrope trek to equality is the one that marches and chants 'it's easier this way!' how it boils you down. you silly girl.

and even though right there in the middle of that ever-so-indie coffee shop you want to turn over tables and shout feminist imposter! and lipstick misogynist! and insipid bitch! this time you don't. sometimes the revolution doesn't break down the door kicking and screaming wearing steel-toed doc martens of truth. sometimes the revolution sleeps on the same side of the bed every night, unsuspicious. makes watercooler conversation like a pro – careful, calculated, patient, patient. rides the elevator with the rest. waits steady. smiles politely. not an advocate for apathy but for strategy, not always but sometimes, not sometimes but this time, so listen to me, girl: when you get to the top, when you arrive at that perfectly polished floor, you shatter it. and maybe that means you're going to take a hit too. you shatter it, you hit hard, until all that's left is the glittering shards of wreckage, the kind that leaves slivers, the kind of slivers that can't be so easily removed.

when you leave i want the world to still be itching at the slicing cut memories of what you did here. when you leave this world i want our daughters to still be rubbing away the glitter from their eyes. and when they start making plans like we once did, when they start casting their gaze upward: no ceiling only sky, no ceiling only sky.

HERE'S HOW

here's how a hundred birds are hanging on the telephone lines of my mouth and here's how they flock away into a sound that is blinding. here's how your voice blinds me. here's how we wake bleary-eyed at 6 to catch the early train and here's how we sleep an entire weekend away. here's how the sun wakes the sky. here's how we eat peanut butter sandwiches in our underwear. here is our dirty dish portrait of intimacy. here's how we watch the neighbors' apartment burn and burn and here's how the smoke snakes the horizon. here are my shaking hands. here's how you hold them, how you whisper songs into the gutters of me. here's how we kiss our way through the cherry popsicle brain freeze. here's how we recite the alphabet backwards to sleep. here are the islands in you i have yet to explore and here are the islands in the atlantic just barely escaping my reach. here's how we can never keep track of the keys. here's how you are more beautiful than anything in the rain. here are all of your syllables distracting me. here's how we get homesick for stargazing when we're in the city. here is the place where you first nervously touch my knee. here's how we get lost at sea. here's how we get and we get and we.

E-MONEYYYY
@itseescott

kids rioting in the streets, setting fire to everything, screaming "MORE OVALTINE!!!"

E-MONEYYYY
@itseescott

whip me with your newborn son's umbilical cord

E-MONEYYYY
@itseescott

this world is really cool but also really fucked up

E-MONEYYYY
@itseescott

i asked my grandmother if she thought i was silly for thinking that we could use poetry to change the world, she said "no, you're brave."

e.e. scott was born in 1991 and currently lives at boost house in maine. she is passionate about ending the culture of dehumanization, empowering young people, and defending planet earth. mostly, she is passionate about her dog.

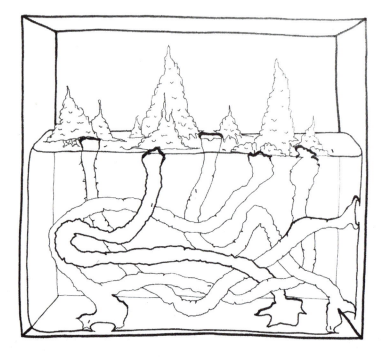

Finally, three months after you made your purchase, the first vial of ants will arrive and be dead. You'll email and call them six more times before the second vial will arrive. The second vial will arrive and 5 of 16 ants will be dead. You'll see them try to dig into the gel to no avail. When the 'colony' arrived in the US it had no inhabitants, no ants. This was not made clear on the website. My daughter-in-law had to fork out to populate it. They are tunneling and interacting and no one can pass by without stopping to watch. Not sure how long they last but it's been fun so far! This is not only nature learning, it is art. Very cool........ I really didn't think they would do anything, but they did! The next morning they had some nice tunnels going and were hard at work. I wouldn't ever buy this on my own, or as a gift for anyone, but it wasn't too bad. They did a great job tunneling through the gel but it looks as if they were drowning in the gel, getting stuck and dying. Our ants also seemed to be killing each other.

200

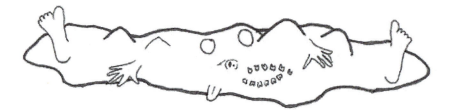

rachel younghans was born in 1989 and currently lives at boost house in maine. an airbrush artist and trained mapmaker, she has airbrushed over 4,000 tshirts in the last three years. rachel visits walmart at least twice a week but doesn't buy anything. one of her favorite times waking up was when a buck woke her up with his antlers.

ADEFISAYO ADEYEYE
papercranechronicles.tumblr.com

BEACH SLOTH
twitter.com/beach_sloth
beachsloth.blogspot.com/
beachsloth.tumblr.com/

GABBY BESS
gabbybess.com
twitter.com/seemstween

LIZ BOWEN
liz-bowen.com
facebook.com/liz.bowen
twitter.com/lizbowhunter
instagram.com/lizbowhunter

MELISSA BRODER
melissabroder.com
twitter.com/melissabroder

JOS CHARLES
joscharles.tumblr.com
facebook.com/jos.d.charles
themlit.com

RICHARD CHIEM
richardchiem.blogspot.com
richardchiem.tumblr.com
twitter.com/giganticanovel

SANTINO DELA
twitter.com/santinodela
instagram.com/santinodela

BRIAN ECKLUND
brianecklund.tumblr.com
twitter.com/classic_bagel

PANCHO ESPINOSA
twitter.com/borntochill

JOSHUA JENNIFER ESPINOZA
blankslate.tumblr.com
facebook.com/joshua.espinoza
.982292
twitter.com/sadqueer4life

CATALINA GALLAGHER
twitter.com/weird_bug

JAMES GANAS
facebook.com/james.ganas
jamesganas.tumblr.com
ask.fm/jamesganas

CEAN GAMALINDA
facebook.com/thoseareballs

CASSANDRA GILLIG
cassandragillig.tumblr.com
twitter.com/cassandragillig

AMELIA GILLIS
exeyeyeye.tumblr.com
themalllitmag.tumblr.com
twitter.com/ameeliagillis

LARA GLENUM
facebook.com/lara.glenum

PHILIP GORDON
twitter.com/greymusic_
grey-music.tumblr.com

TOM HANK
facebook.com/tomhankthatsme
twitter.com/tomhankthatsme

MICHAEL HESSEL-MIAL
twitter.com/mikehesselmial

@HORSE_EBOOKS
twitter.com/horse_ebooks

BRETT ELIZABETH JENKINS
brettejenkins.blogspot.com
facebook.com/brett.e.jenkins
twitter.com/fartmaster5000
instagram.com/cursivewriting
brettjenkins.tumblr.com

RAYMOND JOHNSON
hellopoetry.com/raymond-johnson/
twitter.com/blaxstronaut
instagram.com/blaxstronaut

soundcloud.com/blaxstronaut

KENJI KHOZOEI
facebook.com/kenji.khozoei
kenjikhozoei.tumblr.com/
twitter.com/mfkenji
instagram.com/mfkenji

JI YOON LEE
radioactivemoat.com/imma.html

TAO LIN
taolin.info
twitter.com/tao_lin

CAYLA LOCKWOOD
ohyesitsladiesnight.tumblr.com
caylalockwood.com

PATRICIA LOCKWOOD
twitter.com/tricialockwood

CARRIE LORIG
carrieabigstick.tumblr.com
facebook.com/carrielorig

SHARON MESMER
dubiouslabia.wordpress.com
twitter.com/SharonMesmer

STEPHEN MICHAEL MCDOWELL
newhive.com/buttercup
bit.ly/smmwrt
mammalhabitat.com

LUNA MIGUEL
lunamiguel.com

K. SILEM MOHAMMAD
lime-tree.blogspot.com

MOON TEMPLE
moontempleuniverse.com
twitter.com/mntmpl
facebook.com/thisismyblogurl

ASHLEY OPHEIM
twitter.com/hologramrainbow
ashleyobscura.tumblr.com/
thisishappeningwhetheryou
    likeitornot.bigcartel.com

soundcloud.com/peyotiki

HUNTER PAYNE.
huntermadeit.com
twitter.com/huntermadeit

ANTHONY PEREGRINE
anthonyperegrine.tumblr.com
twitter.com/twanethon
facebook.com/anthony.betori

@POSTCRUNK
twitter.com/postcrunk
postcrunk.bandcamp.com

JOHN ROGERS
cargocollective.com/johnrogers
twitter.com/brainlove
johnbrnlvrogers.tumblr.com
facebook.com/johnbrainlove

AMY SAUL-ZERBY
amysaulzerby.com
facebook.com/amysaulzerby

BOB SCHOFIELD
bobschofield.tumblr.com
twitter.com/anothertower

LK SHAW
lkshow.biz
twitter.com/lkshowbiz
shabbydollhouse.com

ANGELA SHIER
angelashier.tumblr.com
twitter.com/angelashier
instagram.com/angmeeow
snapchat: angmeeow
themallmag.tumblr.com

BIANCA SHIPTON
twitter.com/grarrrrish

ALLI SIMONE DEFEO
roundethings.tumblr.com
alexandraa-simone.tumblr.com

ANDREW W.K.
facebook.com/andrewwk

twitter.com/andrewwk

SARA WOODS
moonbears.biz
whatmountains.tumblr.com
twitter.com/whatmountains

DYLAN YORK
twitter.com/ydylan

CHARLIE THE DOG EMERITUS
instagram.com/dogemeritus

JOSEPH KENDRICK
facebook.com/josephxkendrick
josephxkendrick.tumblr.com
youtube.com/josephxkendrick
twitter.com/josephxkendrick
instagram.com/josephxkendrick

STEVE ROGGENBUCK
steveroggenbuck.com
youtube.com/steveroggenbuck
twitter.com/steveroggenbuck
livemylief.tumblr.com
instagram.com/steveroggenbuck

E.E. SCOTT
twitter.com/itseescott
instagram.com/itseescott

RACHEL YOUNGHANS
rachelyounghans.com
imme.us
responsibiliti.tumblr.com
instagram.com/responsibiliti